DEMCO

Beetles

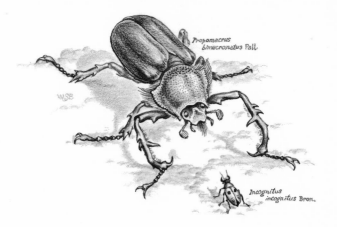

Propomacrus
bimucronatus Pall.

Incognitus
incognitus Bron.

by the same author

THE WONDER WORLD OF ANTS

THE CHISEL-TOOTH TRIBE

CHILDREN OF THE SEA

HORNS AND ANTLERS

STOOPING HAWK AND STRANDED WHALE

THE GRASSHOPPER BOOK

HOOKER'S HOLIDAY

TURTLES

COYOTES

STARLINGS

CATS

FREEDOM AND PLENTY: OURS TO SAVE

GOATS

BEETLES

Written and illustrated by
Wilfrid S. Bronson

Harcourt, Brace & World, Inc.
New York

Library of Congress Catalog Card Number: 63-15397
Printed in the United States of America
D.10.66

Whirligig Beetles ("Writes-My-Name ")L.S.
Gyrinus borealis lugens Lec.

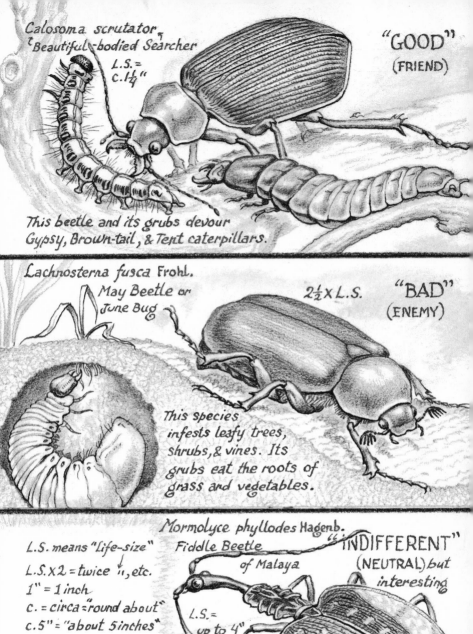

Calosoma scrutator,
"Beautiful-bodied Searcher"
L.S. = c. 1¼"

"GOOD"
(FRIEND)

This beetle and its grubs devour
Gypsy, Brown-tail, & Tent caterpillars.

Lachnosterna fusca Frohl.
May Beetle or
June Bug

2½ × L.S.

"BAD"
(ENEMY)

This species
infests leafy trees,
shrubs, & vines. Its
grubs eat the roots of
grass and vegetables.

L.S. means "Life-size"
L.S. × 2 = twice ", etc.
1" = 1 inch
c. = circa = "round about"
c. 5" = "about 5 inches"
1" = c. 2.54 centimeters
   or 25.4 millimeters
♂ means "male"
♀ means "female"
sp. = "species"

Mormolyce phyllodes Hagenb.
Fiddle Beetle
of Malaya

"INDIFFERENT"
(NEUTRAL) but
interesting

L.S. =
up to 4"

This sp.
lives flatly
under the bark of
fallen jungle trees.

Part One

MACHINES-PLUS

What good is a book about beetles? What good are beetles, anyway? Well, a book about beetles is good because it tells anyone who wants to know what good beetles are, which kinds are good, which are bad, and which are neither good nor bad but very interesting for all that, and explains how all the different kinds live successfully in a world that is very dangerous for insects. Of course, when we ask if a certain beetle is "good" or "bad," we mean is it helpful or harmful to human beings. We are not thinking of what may be good or bad for beetles, any more than they ever think whether they are a boon or a bother to us.

Beetles and other insects don't ask themselves such questions. They just try to go on living as they learned to live long before there were any people to plague or please. But we, the people, can puzzle these things out. We can answer our own questions from the human side and sometimes even from the insect's side, the beetle's side. To do that, to see things as beetles see them, we need to know as much as possible about them, how their bodies are built and how they work and how their minds work too.

Before we learn how each special kind of beetle lives, the helpful and the harmful, it might be a good idea to take one apart and see what makes it "tick," pretty much in the manner of a boy with an old clock. Some beetles really do tick and click quite loudly; and they do remind us of small machines, with their shiny hard surfaces, their hooks and hinges, and the mechanical way they move about.

But living creatures are not merely machines. They are organisms. An organism is an organized body that is alive, as no machine (however well assembled and remarkable) can ever be. An organism is a creature so organized in its many parts that it can feed itself, protect itself, grow, reproduce itself, and finally perhaps feed and protect its offspring. So, as we note the machine-like qualities of beetles, let us remember that insects are not truly machines but are machines-plus.

They are machines with the added ability to operate themselves, to refuel themselves, to repair themselves, yes, and to produce new machines-plus, each insect its own model, the same style year after year. Also year after year for many years, the entomologists (students of insect life) have disagreed as to whether or not these self-operating machines have minds and feelings. Some seem to have assumed that insects have far more mentality and sensibility than they really do, while others go equally too far in asserting that insects, despite brains and nerves, have no minds or feelings at all.

There is a difference of opinion between entomologists on the one side who believe that, whereas human beings (most of them, that is) live by using their intelligence, insects are guided through life entirely by their instincts; and those students on the other side who have satisfied themselves by tests and experiments that insects (some of them, that is) do have, besides instincts, their own small share of intelligence.

Take the case of a pair of Scavenger Beetles, balked in efforts to move their cow-dung ball of provisions because an entomologist pierced and pinned it to the ground with a

8

First, finding their ball immobilized, they tried heaving under it, an instinctive action that usually would move it over ordinary obstructions.

But (the ball only sliding up the stake) they next tried a method more intelligent. With

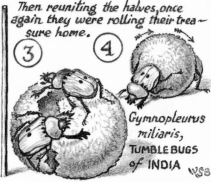

AFTER ILLUSTRATIONS of the EXPERIMENT by MAJOR R.W.G. HINGSTON, M.C.

spike-edged faces & forelegs, they bisected the ball, thus freeing it from the stake.

Then reuniting the halves, once again they were rolling their treasure home.

Gymnopleurus miliaris, TUMBLE BUGS of INDIA

small, smooth stake. The beetles tried inherited instinctive methods to no avail, heaving with their shoulders under the ball, which only slid higher on the stake. Finally they cut the ball in two, put the now free halves together again, and rolled it home. They learned to solve their problem in a new, apparently intelligent way.

Intelligent people can remember and think and learn from experience. They understand about cause and effect — what they must do to bring about a desired result. They also can judge whether their plan is good, and if not, they can change it. All this is the exercise of intelligence. What then is instinct? "Instinct" is a name that men have made up the more easily to argue about something that (for all their own intelligence) they still do not fully understand. In fact, we could say that instinct is really the name of one kind of intelligence, of knowledge ready-stored in the minds of "the lower animals," although man (the highest and most mental animal) also has his own share of instinctive ways.

Instinct is not personal knowledge; it is not something gained in one creature's lifetime from its own experience. It is racial or inherited knowledge, gained by a race of creatures through ages of experience, a kind of built-in know-how born in every member of that race, as much a part of them from the start as any part of their bodies. Each member in its turn knows how to do things — necessary for its own success and for preserving its race — the first time it tries without being taught or seeing it done by others.

Take, for example, the mere matter of moving about. A fly only a few minutes old can walk, easily managing six legs at once — even upside down on the ceiling — whereas a human baby on the floor below must crawl for weeks before it discovers how to stand and walk on its two legs. The insect comes into the world with the instinct and inherited ability to walk. The human newcomer has an instinctive wish to walk, but he has to learn how by trying, by profiting from his mistakes, by using intelligence.

Some scientists feel sure that insects cannot learn anything new, that they cannot alter their inborn ways to solve a problem members of their race have never had to solve before. But there are less intelligent and more intelligent insects, and some of the latter have satisfied other scientists that they can size up a puzzling situation never faced by their kind before and do something intelligent about it. Intelligent creatures must be able to find new and possibly better ways of doing things. Human beings have this ability. But — in a degree suitable to their size and bodily make-up — so do various kinds of ants and wasps and certain other insects, especially some of the scavenger beetles.

And what about feelings? The argument is still the same; those who claim that insects have no minds also argue that insects cannot possibly have feelings either. Other observers and experimenters contradict this. Perhaps it is partly a disagreement as to the meaning of the words "mind" and "feelings." There are feelings of the mind and feelings of the body. You can be unhappy in your mind or uncomfortable in your body. You can have your feelings hurt or you can sit on a tack, or both.

A wasp will buzz a man who gets too close to her nest, and if he doesn't go away, she will sting him. Instead of saying "instinct," some scientists call her performance "inherited behavior." When the man waves his arms and shies away, instead of "intelligence" they call it "learned behavior" because, at birth, he didn't know a wasp could hurt him. Call it by whatever name, both wasp and man will act in such a situation with a show of feeling, whether they have "inherited" or "learned" their behavior. Indeed, it is necessary for each to have feelings about the other before either of them acts at all.

In this book we are not taking sides in this old debate. We shall simply tell what various beetles do and allow you to form your own opinion. One's own opinion is something nobody is obliged to share with anybody else.

Possibly the light of instinct that guides the course of so many creatures shines more brightly at the highest level, grading upward into the power to think and reason, and shades downward more dimly in the darkness of the merest automatic machine-like actions of creatures on lower levels. Yet, though they are machine-like, insects, however lowly,

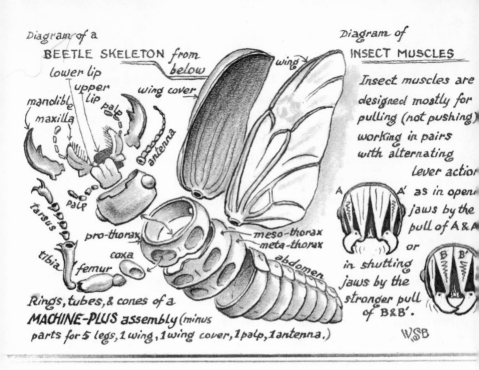

Diagram of a BEETLE SKELETON *from below*

lower lip
upper lip
mandible
maxilla
palp
wing cover
wing
antenna
palp
tarsus
tibia
femur
coxa
pro-thorax
meso-thorax
meta-thorax
abdomen

Rings, tubes, & cones of a
MACHINE-PLUS assembly (minus
parts for 5 legs, 1 wing, 1 wing cover, 1 palp, 1 antenna.)

Diagram of INSECT MUSCLES

Insect muscles are designed mostly for pulling (not pushing) working in pairs with alternating lever action

A   A' as in opening jaws by the pull of A & A' or in shutting jaws by the stronger pull of B & B'.

WSB

Mechanics of a Beetle Leg: **1** = muscle that pulls on tendon **1^x**, that threads foot segments like beads and raises foot (tarsus) in walking.
2 = muscle to pull foot down and clinch claws on objects & surfaces.
3 & 3^x = muscles attached to shin (tibia) that alternately swing it out or in.
4 = muscle that aids 3^x in ····· 3 ·····folding shin on thigh (femur).

COXA   6   7   1   8   TIBIA   1^x
5   3^x FEMUR   2   TARSUS
4

5 = muscle used in raising thigh. **6** = Roller bearing hip (coxa) that swings entire leg fore or aft in its socket on the thorax. **7** = simple hinge for femur.
8 = Offset hinge for tibia.

WSB

are, as we have said, not machines but machines-plus. And beetles seem to illustrate this fact most aptly.

12

In their various styles, beetles make us think of cars and planes, power shovels, cannons, motorboats, and submarines. But for all their outward differences in appearance and performance, all are put together on the same general plan, with variations. The plan includes several systems that we shall look into separately.

SYSTEM I concerns the chassis or the skeleton and muscles of an insect. A beetle's skeleton, the hard and rigid part that supports all the rest, is not inside, as our bones are, but on the outside. This makes a very strong skeleton for the amount of material in it, a skeleton that is also a suit of armor. It is a complicated assembly of joined rings and tubes, all made of a hard and springy stuff called *chitin* (pronounced ki-tin), more like horn or fingernail than like bone or metal. A ring or hollow tube is much harder to bend than a solid rod or ribbon of the same amount of stuff. Try to bend, in your two hands, an eight-inch length of three-quarter-inch copper water-pipe. You can't. Yet the same amount of copper in the form of a heavy wire would be quite pliable. A plain band finger ring keeps its shape for years even on the hand of a machinist engaged in heavy work. But if cut through, it can be bent between your fingers.

The rings of a beetle's skeleton-armor support and protect its body. A beetle, being an insect, is in "sect-ions," a row of rings in three sections. The first several rings are welded solidly together, forming the first section, the head. The next three rings also are welded and form the chest, the second section or thorax. The rest of the body rings are held together only by a tough skinlike tissue, but they overlap each other, each ring fitting into the next, like the tubes of a telescope. They form the third section, the abdomen, which can be shortened or extended (like a telescope) or raised, lowered, or turned from side to side. The body rings are further strengthened by thickened ridges in the armor or by the armor's being folded in various ways and by having all its rims and edges doubled over, much as is the sheet metal of the hood, fenders, top, and trunk cover on your car. The legs are sets of jointed tubes, and the wings are supported by braces, slender and flexible but also hollow and therefore stronger than they would be otherwise. Legs and wings are moved by muscles in the thorax.

Having a hollow skeleton is one reason why beetles, ants, and some other insects are so much stronger for their size than people are. Can any husky muscle-man lift and carry, for a mile or so, something ten times as heavy as himself? First of all, a two-hundred-pound man has to carry his own weight. With two thousand pounds added to that, say a one-ton truck on his shoulder, he couldn't stagger a step. But the weight of a big beetle, in spite of its hefty look, is very little. Ten times very little isn't very much, so insects frequently perform feats of strength that may amaze us.

An insects's muscles are all inside its outside skeleton. Unlike our muscles, which are attached to various rods (our bones), a beetle's muscles have, in proportion, about three times as much room for firm attachment inside its hollow skeleton. The tone and quality of this muscle is about the same as ours. Yet, to take a step, a big beetle needs only to move three of its light legs an inch, whereas a man must move an immensely heavier leg about thirty times that far. No wonder, compared to people, many insects seem to have such super strength and so much power to spare.

In walking, a beetle, having six jointed legs, as do all adult insects, first puts forward the fore and hind legs on its left side and, at the same time, the middle leg on its right. It sets these down and advances the other three, the right fore and hind legs and the left middle leg. This method of walking keeps the weight always on a steady, ever moving alternating tripod. The legs are attached to its body by a sort of ball-and-socket arrangement, which may not allow as much freedom as our shoulder joints do. But the other joints in its legs are hinged, each facing a different way, making it easy for a beetle to do a wide variety of things with its feet and legs, from climbing trees or digging holes or moving loads to cleaning its body and washing its face. Yet its method of locomotion is mechanically so simple that it has been possible to make large wind-up toy beetles that walk exactly like the natural animal.

There is nothing simple about a beetle's flying. It is a more complicated performance than the flight of most other insects. That some of the heavier, more oddly shaped beetles actually can fly is hard to believe. But most of them can and do. True, they fly clumsily, inefficiently, and noisily, but it is surprising that they can take off at all. What aircraft designer in his right mind would plan a fuselage so top-heavy with projecting parts that it must tear a jagged path instead of slipping smoothly through the air?

The turbulence in the air must be terrific around one of the more oddly built beetles in flight. Its roly-poly body has no tail assembly and no rudder. So it pitches drunkenly and veers from its course, only to swerve back onto it again, often seeming to fly without controls of any kind. Yet the great bumbling fellow does get to where it wants to go. It may steer by altering the angle of its wing strokes and shifting the weight a little, perhaps with its legs, and possibly by slight changes in the tilt of its wing covers. These seem to lock in a raised position, like the trunk cover on a car, but there is room about the hinges for plenty of play.

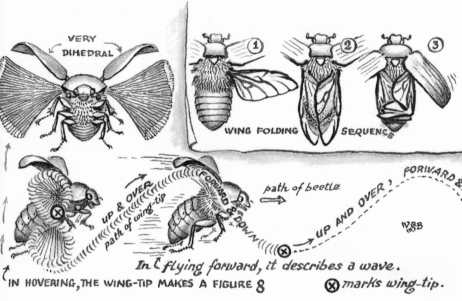

VERY DIHEDRAL

① ② ③

WING FOLDING SEQUENCE

path of beetle

UP & OVER path of wing-tip FORWARD & DOWN

UP AND OVER FORWARD & D

path of beetle

WSB

In flying forward, it describes a wave.

IN HOVERING, THE WING-TIP MAKES A FIGURE 8 ⊗ marks wing-tip.

The wing covers are actually a beetle's first pair of wings, heavily plated with chitin. They are the armor that protects a beetle's back and the far lighter second pair of wings when all are folded down. This lighter second pair provides the power of flight. They are the beetle's propellers. But they don't revolve like a plane's propellers because the beetle is, after all, not actually a machine. The wings whir, but they don't whirl. Whirling would wring them right off the beetle.

A wheel or propeller can revolve or be removed and replaced. It is a separate piece of a machine. But a leg or a wing or any other living part must remain attached to the animal. So, in order not to twist them off, the beetle, instead of twirling its wings in complete circles, makes figure eights, turning unfinished circles back on each other. This you can see when it hovers or flies in one place. When flying ahead, it is still making figure eights, but they become a series of wavy scallops. In the illustration see how the figure eight becomes one crest and one trough of a wave when drawn out, as a beetle, moving forward, extends the pattern of its hovering motions.

As the wings make their own waves, they get support from the air while striking forward and down and while rising to the crest of the next stroke forward and down. On the forward and down stroke, the beetle speeds ahead like a surfboard rider on an ocean wave. There is an instant when its wings strike backward, and then, on the upstroke, it is supported and continues forward like a kite pulled by a running boy.

At this point, though the beetle may look too heavy to fly at all, its weight may even be a help, for this carries the beetle forward while the wings are rising to make the next downstroke. A lighter insect, like a butterfly, bobs up and down on bigger wings and is quickly blown off course by a little breeze. It is the same thing when you throw a baseball and a tennis ball or a golf ball and a ping-pong ball. The weight and propulsion of the solid balls carry them farther than you can throw the light ones.

You may read in most books and articles about beetles that the first pair of wings, the chitin-coated wing covers, "are of no use in flight." But this is probably incorrect. When they fly, the different kinds of beetles raise their wing covers at whatever angle suits them best (out of the way of the whirring second pair, the propeller wings) and hold them as rigidly in place as the wings of airplanes.

The wing covers are very much like a plane's wings in at least two ways and may be of more use to a flying beetle than is usually assumed. Firstly, they are concave below and convex above. This arrangement could give a helpful lift, once the propeller wings get up speed. And secondly, they are very dihedral, that is, they rise above the beetle at an angle, almost in a V on some kinds. This would seem to be the only stabilizing apparatus most beetles have. It helps them to keep their balance, not to tip too far to one side or the other.

One of the biggest, burliest beetles, the great African Goliath (*Goliathus goliathus* Drury), which hardly raises its wing covers at all, is believed to have developed its own gyroscopes, similar in their use to those spinning devices in planes and ships that help to keep them upright in rough going, as a top is held upright by its own whirling. Goliath twists and turns his legs while on the wing. So perhaps after all, a beetle's flying apparatus isn't necessarily as "impossible" as it may look.

Of course, not all beetles are so heavily built that they must blunder through the air like "flying boxcars." Some kinds are as quick and light on the wing as a fly. But almost all beetles, including the long-bodied kinds, have to unfold their even longer propeller wings to fly and, after alighting, fold them up again and tuck them back under the wing covers for safety's sake. Some other insects fold their wings in simple ways, but the folding of a beetle's wings is very complex and hard to understand.

First the wings are laid back along the body, their trailing edges overlapping. Then the leading edges, together with the nearest forward portions of the wings, are folded lengthwise. But this procedure leaves their outer ends — almost half the wing's length on a May beetle — projecting beyond the body unprotected. So now, in a third movement, these delicate outer ends must also be folded under the wing covers.

It has puzzled many students to know by what means the outer ends are finally tucked under after the wings are laid over the back and folded lengthwise. There are no ligaments or cords that can draw up the ends while folding them fanwise across the beetle's back. The thin transparent membrane of the wings is supported by the slender but strong and springy braces, somewhat as the cloth of an umbrella is spread and supported by its ribs. In most flying insects the braces run the full length of the wings. But because a beetle's wing must be doubled under itself, there are joints in the braces to allow it.

Notice in the illustration those two big braces in the forward half of the wing. They seem to have their tips bent part way back just even with the joint on the leading edge. Are the tips held open under tension by the strength of the shoulder muscles, which stretch out the entire wing? Do the tips strain steadily to lie parallel along the braces? When the shoulder muscles have relaxed completely, do these spring-like tips (now free to close) draw up the outer ends of the

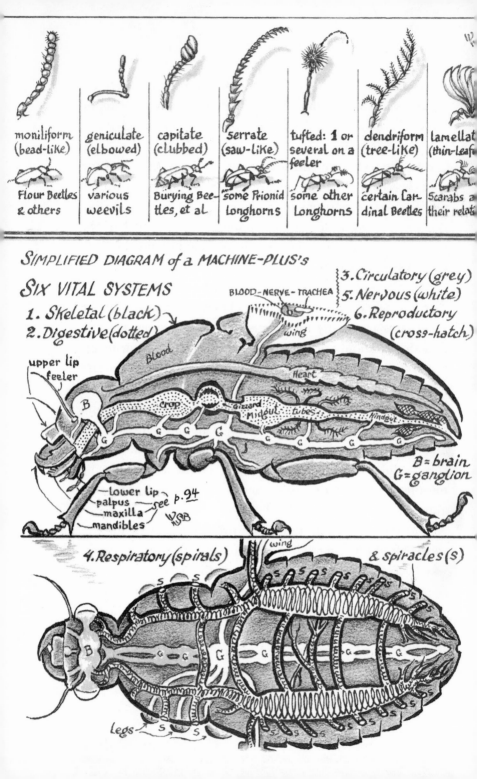

moniliform
(bead-like)

Flour Beetles
& others

geniculate
(elbowed)

various
weevils

capitate
(clubbed)

Burying Bee-
tles, et al

serrate
(saw-like)

some Prionid
Longhorns

tufted: **1** or
several on a
feeler

some other
Longhorns

dendriform
(tree-like)

certain Car-
dinal Beetles

lamellat
(thin-leaf

Scarabs a
their relati

SIMPLIFIED DIAGRAM of a MACHINE-PLUS's

SIX VITAL SYSTEMS

BLOOD - NERVE - TRACHEA

1. Skeletal (black)
2. Digestive (dotted)

3. Circulatory (grey)
5. Nervous (white)
6. Reproductory
   (cross-hatch)

upper lip
feeler

Blood

wing

B

crop

Heart

Gizzard
Midgut   tubes

Hindgut

G   G   G

G

G

B = brain
G = ganglion

lower lip
palpus — see p. 94
maxilla
mandibles

WSB

4. Respiratory (spirals)   wing   & spiracles (s)

S   S   S   S   S   S   S

B

G   G   G   G   G

S

S   S   S

legs   S   S   S   S   S   S

wings, already creased to fold like a paper fan?

Just beyond the springy tips, do you see that open area of membrane, of transparent wing material? It doesn't stretch out taut like the rest of the wing; there is more than enough material to cover the spot. Maybe this extra material is necessary to allow for the two-way folding at that point, first lengthwise, then crosswise. Perhaps the muscles that move the leading edge of the wings (now lying along the back) relax completely only after the lengthwise folding. Wouldn't this let the outer edge of the wing slip back a little farther, thus aiding the crosswise folding by a gentle leverage?

Scientists as yet don't know all about the folding of the wings. It is one of many questions concerning beetles, their lives and habits, that may be fully answered some day, not necessarily by trained professionals but, quite possibly, by young amateur observers with very sharp eyes. So much for SYSTEM I — the chassis or fuselage and devices for travel.

SYSTEM II deals with fuel and engine, the food and digestion of an insect. Like cars and planes, a living machine must be repeatedly refueled, or fed, to keep it going. Gasoline is the food of cars and planes; food is the fuel of our little "machines-plus," the beetles. Like the smaller types of cars, these little machines-plus run longer on less fuel than larger kinds of creatures can.

A beetle has a crop into which the food goes first. A car has a fuel tank.

A beetle has a stomach to digest the food, thus obtaining energy. A car has a motor that burns the gas, converting it to horsepower.

A beetle has an intestine or a "hind-gut." A car has an exhaust and a tail pipe.

But a beetle's digestion is more complicated than a car's. The car's fuel comes ready to burn. It has been well prepared at the refinery. The beetle has to refine its own fuel, to select and chew its food and mix it with an "additive," its saliva, before taking any into its crop and stomach. For this necessary work the beetle seems to have a face full of gadgets. It has three pairs of feelers, one pair on its face and two pairs as parts of its mouth, which, with its two pairs of jaws, form a complex assembly of tools before and all about its gullet.

The most noticeable feelers, mounted between or in front of a beetle's eyes, are called the antennae. They are for testing things by touch, and they may help a beetle hear, though no one can say that they are its ears. At their bases there is an area that is said to be sensitive to sound vibrations. So are the radio antennae on a car. But mainly the messages received from the air are gathered by a sense of smell in the beetle's antennae, most useful in locating mates and finding food.

Somewhat as the television antennae on our houses vary from roof to roof, beetle antennae are of many different designs, from simple to extremely fancy and elaborate. And as one type of antennae may bring in our preferred programs better than another, so probably each special design of feeler is better able to pick up the scents of mates and food especially sought by each kind of beetle.

The jaws of beetles open sideways instead of up and down like ours, making it mechanically workable to have two pairs between the upper and lower lips. The bigger, simpler, but

22

more eye-catching jaws, the mandibles, are just above and in front of the creature's gullet. The smaller but more complicated jaws, the maxillae, are just below the mandibles, one on each side of the gullet. The big mandibles, with sharp edges and pointed teeth, are designed for snatching and holding, for piercing and tearing and cutting up its prey if the beetle is a carnivore — a meat eater — or for biting chunks out of plants if it is an herbivore — a vegetable feeder. The maxillae also have hard cutting edges to help shred the food more finely, plus one of the two pairs of mouth feelers (called palps or palpi) for holding and tasting the food and moving it about in the mouth. On the maxillae also is mounted a pair of stiff combs, which, coming together, may screen out all bits of food not yet small enough to be swallowed. The other two palpi are one on each side of the lower lip.

The food gets well shredded in the mouth; yet even after it is swallowed, it will be ground still more thoroughly. A beetle's digestion takes place in a flexible and elastic tube that runs through the animal from end to end, expanded in places and with various organs attached to it along the way. Bits of swallowed food go first into the crop, an expanded area, where they are formed into a pellet that passes on and into the *pro-ven-tri-cu-lus,* a scientist's word merely meaning the "fore-gut." It is really a sort of gizzard, being lined with ridges covered with chitinous teeth. Special muscles move these ridges in such a way that the already shredded bits in the pellet are milled very fine while being mixed with digestive fluids.

Passing next into the mid-gut, the food is drenched with more digestive fluids which flow all through it, dissolving every atom of the finely ground stuff. From this wet mixture, the blood, which envelopes all the beetle's "innards," now soaks up nourishment through the mid-gut's porous skin. Finally, when the remaining matter moves into the hind-gut, most of the water in it is reabsorbed and so is not lost as urine.

Attached to the hind-gut is a set of tubes that serves as kidneys, a beetle's fuel filter, extracting impurities from the blood and discharging them into the last part of the long digestive tube to be carried away. Meanwhile, the nourishment, now in the blood, flows all through the beetle's body, repairing worn tissues while the insect rests and providing plenty of power when it is on the move again.

SYSTEM III is the fuel pump and transmission, an insect's heart and circulation.

To deliver a beetle's fuel — the nourishment in its blood — to all parts of the body, there is a fuel pump — the heart. But except for one main artery from the heart to the brain, the blood is not contained in veins and arteries as is our own. It is everywhere in the beetle, washing freely among the muscles and organs. The heart just keeps it well stirred up. It is helped by the contraction and expansion of the abdomen as the beetle breathes and by any active movements it may make.

The heart of a beetle is an elastic tube that beats just beneath its back, the whole length of the abdomen. It is full of the nearly transparent, pale yellow-green blood and is enveloped by more of the same. It is, in fact, like a submersible pump lying in a lake, pushing through a hose some of the water in which it is submerged. In a beetle, the hose is its one and only artery, leading directly from the heart through the thorax to its head.

Along the sides of the tubular heart are little valves that open to let blood in from the surrounding reservoir but close when the heart contracts, forcing blood forward and bathing the beetle's brain. To this organ, so important in an alert insect, refreshing nourishment flows first. Then the blood seeps back through other areas, bathing and refreshing all the beetle's organs, muscles, and other tissues.

Such a system probably would not work well at all in animals bigger than the biggest insects. To the outer ends of their legs and feelers is about as far as this way of moving blood would reach with good results. Maybe that's why, fortunately, an insect such as a Tiger Beetle is no bigger than a beetle, instead of being as large as a tiger.

This is probably the proper place to answer a question that will occur to anyone who watches living insects such as ants and beetles. When a beetle loses a leg, why doesn't it bleed to death as a tiger would? For one thing, an insect's blood clots more quickly than a mammal's and plugs the leak almost instantly. And think how tiny is the tear it must mend on a beetle compared with the great muscled leg of the tiger. An insect's leg generally breaks off at a joint. It is narrower and weaker there than along its armored shanks. And there may be a little torn flap of skin or chitin that will clog the drain, moved into place at the break by the blood's very pressure. So the little hole is sutured, the self-repair of a small machine-plus quickly done.

If the tiger lived, a long time would pass before he could hobble about, whereas a beetle or other insect can walk away immediately from its accident, almost as well on five legs as on six. There are various kinds of insects that will break off a leg on purpose to escape capture. Pick up a cricket by one hind leg. You will be left holding the leg while the rest of the insect hops and scurries to safety.

Some kinds of beetles seem able to bleed on purpose. When picked up by a bird or a beetle collector, they fold their legs as in death while, from the knee joints in their armor, yellow droplets ooze. But this liquid isn't really blood. It is the special fluid secreted by scent glands that open through tiny tubes in the skin at the joints. When the beetle flexes its upper leg muscles while the knees are bent, they press against these glands (encased with them in the leg armor) and so squeeze out some of the fluid. This teaches a young and inexperienced bird to leave such beetles alone (generally bright-colored beetles like the ladybirds), for the fluid has a horrid odor, a very bitter taste, and will prove to be painfully poisonous if the bird is still foolish enough to swallow it anyhow. On a collector's fingers the scent lasts a long time.

We have said that, except for the big one to the head, a beetle has no arteries or veins to circulate the blood. But now we must point out that blood can only be distributed in the wings through some sort of tubing. The hollow wing braces — often called "wing veins" — provide this, for though they are tiny, there is room in them for the blood, and it gets especially well stirred when most desirable, during flight.

So we see that a beetle's transmission is not mechanical, as in a car. The new energy that nourishment brings (without cranks, gears, or turning wheels) is transmitted directly to running legs and whirring wings by the fuel pump stirring its blood. The fresh power is used up between meals in all the activities of a vigorous little machine-plus.

26

SYSTEM IV deals with air intake and cooling system, an insect's breathing.

Nourishment, fuel or food, isn't all that is needed to produce power and energy, to provide for the running of a car or the upkeep of a creature. Air must be added. An engine won't burn the finest fuel, nor can an animal make any use of its food, without air. Both the engine's spark of fire and an animal's spark of life will quickly die for lack of air. Air is a mixture of gases, the most important to animals and engines being oxygen. An engine gets oxygen through its carburetor. A creature gets oxygen through its breathing.

There are various ways of breathing, but all are alike in one thing. Air with its oxygen must be brought to some part of a creature's body, inside or out, where the skin is so very thin and delicate that oxygen gas can pass through it, though blood will not. The air is on one side of the thin membrane; the moving blood in the animal is on the other. The blood draws purifying, life-preserving oxygen in through the thin, porous skin and gives out through the skin a poisonous waste gas called carbon dioxide (carbonic acid gas), which is exhaled.

In warm-blooded creatures such as birds and mammals, the thin, porous membrane is in the lungs. In cold-blooded animals such as sea snails and fishes, it is in the gills. But except for a few kinds of larvae (lar-vee), their immature wormlike stages, insects have neither gills nor lungs. An insect's breathing apparatus consists of still another system of tubing that reaches into every part of its body.

The tubes for air in an insect are called tracheae (tra-ke-ee). They are not stiff like the tubular armor of a beetle's leg. They are flexible though noncollapsible, being wound round and round their whole length with tough springy coils of wiry chitin that keep them open wherever they bend, like the reinforcing wire coils in heavy rubber hoses.

Two main air tubes or tracheae reach from one end of an insect to the other, like the trunks of twin trees. Smaller tracheae spread out and out from these, ever more finely, as from trunk to boughs to branches to tiniest twigs. These tiniest twigs, called tracheoles, loop out from the smallest tracheae tips like the outlines of leaves. As we have seen, blood reaches the full length of a beetle's wings through the hollow braces, moved by the heart, aided by contractions of the abdomen, whose several wide rings slip a little way in and out of each other like the tubes of a telescope. But this bellows action is mainly for pumping air through the tracheae that spread in the blood all through the body and legs and braces of the wings. Wherever blood moves in the beetle, air is carried in tubular tracheae to refresh it.

How fanciful Nature seems to have been with her use of tubes in designing insects! Tubular skeleton armor, tubes for defensive "perfume," a tube for digestion, tubes for kidneys, a tubular heart, and air tubes running inside the tubular veins that brace the wings. Tubes, more tubes, and tubes within tubes.

But how does the air get into an insect's two main tracheae in the first place? Not through nostrils or the mouth but through air holes along its sides. On each side of each body ring of the abdomen is a little opening called a spiracle. There are two pairs of spiracles on the thorax as well. By a small tube, each spiracle or air hole connects with the nearer of the two main tubes, which then branch out as already described.

28

Your car has an air cleaner over the carburetor. Just so, the spiracles of an insect may be lined with bristles to sift and clean the air it inhales. They can be closed entirely or opened, as best suits the breathing creature. Up forward, the two pairs of spiracles on the sides of the thorax are somewhat larger than the ones on the abdomen. By closing all the air holes along its abdomen while expanding its body, the beetle draws air in through the holes in its thorax. Then closing these also, it contracts its body, forcing the air into all its parts and finally out through the now open holes in the abdomen. Insects can vary this process as best suits them under changing weather conditions and the amount of energy they are using, it being only necessary to pass air in and out of the abdominal spiracles when they are resting in mild weather.

That is how adult insects breathe, without either lungs or gills. Certain kinds of water beetles in their larval stage do breathe with gills, however. Their gills stand out along their sides, one pair where each pair of spiracles will open when the larva's time comes to go ashore and turn into an adult beetle. Fringed and feathery, they are covered by a very delicate membrane, through which air, but not blood or water, will pass. These spreading gills are full of tiny tracheae into which they draw the air that is dissolved in the water and, like roots of trees, convey it to the trunks, the two main air tubes, whence it goes on into the branches and farthest twigs of the tracheal system. Refreshing oxygen mingles with the nourishment in the blood, bringing new power to the little machine-plus, new energy to the insect.

There are other ways by which underwater larvae get the oxygen they need. Some sluggish kinds simply absorb it through their skins. Certain small beetle larvae have two sharp, curving daggers on their latter ends for stabbing the stems of water lilies. The stems are full of little chambers containing air. At the base of each dagger the larva has a spiracle to press quickly and hold against the punctures in the lily stem. The air, escaping through the punctures, is trapped by these spiracles and passes into the insect's tracheae. And so it breathes air underwater.

Neither of these larvae, the gill breathers or the lily-stabbers, need ever rise to the water's surface for air. But you can see other kinds rising repeatedly to push a tube on their rear ends out of water and draw air into their tracheae. Both the larvae and adults of various water beetles are obliged to do this.

It would seem to be a bothersome way to live, having to go up for air every few minutes. But ages ago various land insects must have found water a safer place to live, or at least an easier place to find food. Gradually adapting their ways to living underwater, they became in time the little self-operating submarines we see today in almost any pond or quiet stream.

Insects are cold-blooded; that is, they have no way of keeping their blood warm when the air grows chilly. So we may say that, with air pumped all through their bodies, they are air-cooled but air-heated too. The colder the air, the colder they are, and the more slowly they move. But the warmer the air, the warmer they become and the better they feel. They grow more alert and active. A cold motor runs better after it is warmed up.

SYSTEM V is concerned with lights and ignition, or the insect's nerves. No motor will run or even start without its electric wiring. And no insect can move or do anything at all without the brain and nerves that induce and control its every action. Like us, a beetle has a brain in its head. But unlike us, instead of having the biggest nerves running down its back as ours do, a beetle's main nerves run along its belly. Our human brains are much more complicated and bigger for our size than a beetle's.

But an insect makes up for some of this difference in the relative size of its brain by having ganglia every so often on its long belly nerves — thickened places like knots in a string, which act as assistant brains. They are nerve centers, centers of control. In the thorax, for example, they give the impulse to wings and legs to move in ways required for doing one thing or another, or to stop moving. Other centers all along an insect's body control the beat of its heart, the digestion of its food, the intake and outgo of its breathing, and so forth.

And yet, in their performance, all these special controls are influenced first by the brain, the biggest nerve center of all, where a creature gets its impressions of what goes on in the world around it. The sudden sight of someone coming toward it may make a beetle fly away. Or it may be so frightened that it lets go of the leaf it is on and drops to the ground, paralyzed and seeming to be dead. In either case it does something — with wings or legs moved by the small unconscious assistant brains in its thorax — because it has sensed danger through the use of its eyes and the big head brain they serve.

Some scientists are sure that the beetle simply "reacts" automatically whenever it sees a large moving shape and does one of the two things just mentioned. It is also asserted that these reactions are not accompanied or promoted by any feelings. But no one has proved that an insect cannot be frightened just because it cannot think. We ourselves react to danger with our feelings and do things without thinking. Again, it may be mainly a difference in our use of words. "Sensing" danger may mean one thing to one person, something else to another.

Take Japanese Beetles. As you approach, they stop eating the leaves of your roses and grow tense, watching to see if you will come "too close for comfort," their hind legs raised stiffly out on either side, quivering like an auxiliary pair of feelers. Should they fly or drop to the lawn? They have a choice of three alternatives common to their kind. If they are only three automatons clustering on a leaf, why does one fly, one drop to the lawn, and the third sit very still? The one on the lawn has yet another choice. It may continue playing possum in plain sight or suddenly "come to life" and scramble more deeply into the grass to hide. What makes the difference in their behavior? Is it just possible that they are individual enough to "make up their own minds"?

A beetle's brain is simple compared to ours. But maybe this is partly a matter of wiring. If we consider the insect's nerves as its electrical connections, we see that they are strung out like cables, farther and farther from the big central power station, the brain. But if all the ganglia, or assistant brains, along their length could be gathered in the insect's head and connected more closely with the brain already there, together they would form a much more complicated brain.

Is it unreasonable to insist that any creature that uses a

brain has a mind of some sort? The brain is only a mind's instrument. No matter how talented you are, to be a violinist, you must have the instrument and you must play it. To be a successful beetle, you need both a brain and a mind to use it. A beetle's mind and a man's mind are surely as unlike as their brains are different in size and structure. Though the beetle may not be able to think the way we think, it is born with its mind ready-stocked with ideas that will fit its needs, ideas that will be generally right enough to guide it through an insect's life. Our human minds are ready-stocked with many of the same ideas. The big difference is in our greater ability to add new and more complicated ideas to those we are born with, to learn and remember more and to think further.

These built-in, ready-made ideas are of course the instincts, the inherited behavior we were discussing earlier. Instincts seldom change. They are ages old. Through its inherited know-how an insect can do some very difficult things and do them very well without being taught or seeing them done by other insects. Instincts don't have to be learned. Along with the necessary tools, an insect is born with the impulse and the ability to use them.

If the mind of a very wise person may be likened to a deep mixing bowl full of thought, seasoned with a pinch of instinct, then an insect's mind is a teaspoonful of instinct salted with at least a grain of thought. It is a sure thing that no beetle can think about its own thinker as we are thinking now! Yet let us not forget that we have in common with beetles and all other animals certain basic needs: for food, for a mate, for safety, for rest, and so on, having also special inborn instinctive ideas for obtaining these things, each according to our kind, our size and structure, and our various dispositions.

Having so many needs in common doesn't make us any more able to understand each other. One person cannot read another person's mind, let alone a beetle's. We can only guess what people or beetles think by what they do. Even then we may guess wrong as to why they do certain things. In spite of having such superior minds (or perhaps because of it), we find it almost as impossible to think like a beetle as for the insect to think like us. (Might we become "beetle-browed" attempting it?)

But again, what about feelings? Do beetles merely react to danger or do they become frightened? Fear is a feeling of the mind. And what about pain? Pain is a feeling of the body. Possibly insects don't feel this kind of hurt as keenly as we do, what with their scattered assistant brains and the quicker healing of their wounds. But just as they show discomfort in being too wet or dry or dusty, surely they feel the extreme discomfort of bodily pain. This is probably best shown when two armies of ants clash in battle. When an ant is wounded, it quickly turns and grasps the injured part in its jaws, much as a man, dancing around in agony, may jab a battered thumb into his mouth after missing the nail with his hammer.

People and beetles, each in their respective ways, experience feelings painful or pleasant, though we may behave differently about them. We both are charmed by things that shine and glitter, from bright chandeliers to the light of the moon, a sky full of stars, or the soft glow of a single candle. People look and like. But as with moths, a beetle may do more. It may fly toward the light and be so bedazzled that it cannot turn aside in time to avoid being burned if the shine is from an open flame such as a candle or a campfire. Lucky is the night-flying beetle that only collides with the lighted window of your home. It is rudely halted but, at its own speed, is not turned into a blob on the window pane as it would be crashing against your windsheld with the car doing sixty.

The attraction some insects feel for lights is called a taxis, a positive taxis. To be charmed by light is a common thing in nature. Certain caterpillars crawl up trees toward the brightest light, the sun. There they find themselves among the newest, tenderest leaves, and they fare far better than they would in the shade below.

We also rise when the light awakens us. And just as surely as a beetle may be burned by a candle's unshielded flame, so the sun can burn and even kill us if we expose ourselves too freely to its rays. Charmed by its light as reflected from the moon, we may become inspired with the most romantic notions, with wishes that can never be fulfilled. May we wonder if moths and beetles ever take off toward the attracting moon, doomed insect astronauts who, though escaping the teeth and beaks of bats and nighthawks, can never reach their lofty goal? Or, instinctively, do they know that it is one light quite beyond their powers of flight?

Of course, we humans can close our eyes to things that are too tempting, whereas insects, having no lids, cannot close their eyes to anything. They cannot roll their eyes, and most kinds are unable to turn their heads very far for a special look at anything, either. But they don't have to wheel about to see on either side and behind them, for their eyes are placed well out on the rounding sides of their heads. Some kinds have such bulging eyes that they can't help seeing in all directions at once all the time.

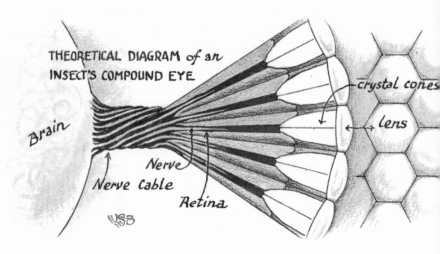

THEORETICAL DIAGRAM of an INSECT'S COMPOUND EYE

crystal cones

lens

Brain

Nerve

Nerve Cable

Retina

WSB

An eye is a "camera-plus," a living camera that catches still and movie shots of whatever is before it, with never a need to change the film. Ever-changing pictures print directly on the film instantaneously and continuously, as long as the eye keeps looking. The film in such a living camera — or "camera-plus" — is called the retina, a membrane very sensitive to changes in the light. To this extent, human and insect eyes are alike. But beyond this, insects have eyes so unlike ours that surely what they see must appear quite differently to them than the same things do to us.

Many insects have two kinds of eyes, simple and compound. Compound eyes are composed of many simple eyes all bunched together and facing out in all directions. The compound eyes are often so big that, as on a fly, they appear to form the whole round head. Between the compound eyes insects may have up to three small and separate simple eyes on the forehead. Many kinds of beetle grubs have simple eyes on the sides of their heads. As adult beetles they have compound eyes but no simple eyes on the forehead.

In a compound eye each simple eye, like a simple box camera, has a lens to focus the view before it on the film we call the retina. Into and through this retina — this living photofilm — penetrate the branching tips of delicate little nerves, like attachments of tiny wires. These all join to form a cable, the big optic nerve, which transmits the views from all the simple eyes in the compound eye to the brain. There all their separate images are registered at once producing a complete panorama of the world around the insect, like the mosaic pictures on a great domed ceiling where the artist has done his work with many small, flat, variously colored stones, instead of using paints and a brush. All the views are blended in the impression they make on the insect's mind. Eyes look, but it is the mind that sees.

At night, an insect that looks in every direction at once has the whole arch of the sky for its personal planetarium. Perhaps it sees all the brighter stars, but surely it will take especial interest in a "shooting star." Except close up, most beetles don't see things as clearly as we do, but like many other animals, they are quick to notice anything that moves. Much nearer than the shooting stars are fireflies on the wing. Seen against a midsummer evening sky, as you lie on the grass to get a worm's-eye view, these two moving lights, the insect's close at hand and the star's far away, appear very similar.

Shooting star glows descending —
Photinus pyralis shines ascending —

Both are likely to be most numerous in the same season of the year, in August. Does the earthbound female firefly, the glowworm, ever mistake one for the other — the meteor for a male firefly overhead — and put forth her brightest gleam, attempting to enchant a shooting star? Firefly and glowworm, they are neither fly nor worm but male and female beetles of a kind that can shine or not, as they choose, and find their mates even in the dark of the moon, each by the other's flashlight.

No matter how smooth and shiny beetles may appear, they are covered with very tiny spines and bristles, some stubby and conelike, some hairlike, simple or feathery, and usually

too small to be seen without a lens or to be felt with the fingers. Each spine projects a short way through a minute hole or pore in the armor and is "hooked up" just inside it to a network of nerves that connect with the brain or one of the assistant brains, thus providing the insect with a sense of touch. They are especially dense on the antennae and palpi, with which a beetle touches things. But when something touches a beetle anywhere on its body, even the smoothest, most polished-looking little machine-plus will feel it and will know. Nerves for the senses of touch, taste, sight, smell, and hearing are all wired up to bring the beetle information and sensations important to its success and satisfaction in a hazardous world.

SYSTEM VI pertains to the manufacture of machines-plus, insect production and distribution.

An insect's production is reproduction. Through the laying of eggs and the growing up of the grubs, their children, they produce themselves again and again, by the hundreds, thousands, or millions, almost never varying the model from year to year or century to century or age to age. Among insects caught in tree pitch millions of years ago (the pitch now hardened into translucent amber), though some kinds are now extinct, many are the same as those living today, so few and trifling have the changes been in all that time.

Grubs of beetles, caterpillars of butterflies, maggots of flies are the common terms applied to various insect larvae. All such larvae are mobile digesting systems, their one preoccupation being food. They eat and grow and store up fat and energy for the great turning point in their lives. In time, as marvelous a change will come to a beetle grub as comes to caterpillars — the crawling worms that turn into butterflies and moths — with a complete altering of appearance and behavior.

Such a seemingly sudden change doesn't come to immature insects of every kind. When grasshoppers hatch from eggs, they are not grubs or worms but small 'hoppers. The main difference from their elders is their winglessness and the bigness of their heads and legs for the size of their bodies — a common trait of baby creatures. A grasshopper baby has already made the big change from its wormlike infant stage to almost the adult form while still inside the egg before hatching, even as each of us changed wonderfully within our mothers, from little fishlike beings with a tail and gills to human babies, before we were born.

But with beetles, butterflies, and many other kinds of insects, the baby hatches while still only a tiny wormlike being. It eats and grows and then makes about itself a new enclosure, an egg-shaped silk cocoon, a plain horny case or chrysalis, or some other little cell or chamber where it can lie completely quiet while the critical time is passed during which it evolves into a grownup insect like its parents. At this inactive stage it is called a pupa, and it is said to be pupating.

The difference is so great between what disappears into the little pupal chamber and what finally comes out that it is called a complete change or "complete metamorphosis," as distinguished from the "incomplete metamorphosis" or changing of a growing grasshopper. The transformation is so astonishing that it seems a miracle and is almost as hard to explain. Indeed, entomologists haven't yet been able clearly to trace the succeeding developments that occur during com-

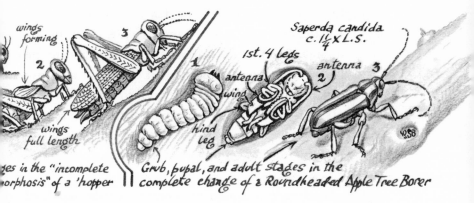

wings
forming

2

3

wings
full length

Saperda candida
c. $1\frac{1}{4}$ *X L.S.*

1st. 4 legs

1

antenna

wing

hind
leg

antenna
2

3

ges in the "incomplete
orphosis" of a 'hopper | | *Grub, pupal, and adult stages in the*
complete change of a Roundheaded Apple Tree Borer

plete metamorphosis. The organs and tissues, all the stuff the
larva is made of, seem just to melt down like lumps of food
in a long-simmering pot. And from this thick living "soup"
the new adult is formed. It breaks out of its cell and comes
forth all grown up, perfect in the minutest detail, still weak
and tender when born this second time, pale and soft except
for its jaws, which are dark and hard enough already for the
taking of food. It will harden and darken all over but will
change no more either in size or style.

The eggs of beetles are laid variously by the different kinds
(or species) on or near a food supply for the grubs that will
hatch, in the shelter of cracks and crevices, rolled up in
leaves, or hidden in chambers bored in wood or tunneled in
the earth.

Ordinarily, soon after mating, the male beetle leaves, never
to return, as does the female also, once her eggs are laid. Less
commonly, the resulting grubs may be fed and cared for
painstakingly by the mother, in some cases with help from
the father beetle also. But most adult insects don't live long
enough to see their own children. When new adults emerge

41

from their changing chambers, the females already have eggs and the males are ready to make them fertile. Then the eggs are laid, and after that the parents die. When the tiny new grubs hatch, they begin at once to eat. They eat and grow, and when they are big grubs, they go into their own pupal chambers to transform into new adults themselves, ready in turn to reproduce the same machines-plus on the same old pattern, long tested and found most usable, patented by Nature millions of years ago.

The distribution of insects has been mostly through a self-delivery service since very early times. Their great-great-grand ancestors crept out of the sea, following the edible plants that had become established on the land. That was the first delivery — delivery ashore — of the first crude insect machine-plus models. Changes were needed, and in those earliest ages, many were made — operational improvements — until the true insect type was finally created.

Changes continued to occur, developing all the different kinds of insects. But the basic underlying insect design was kept, with endless variations of only secondary importance added, just as all makes of automobiles have certain fundamental parts in common, with changes being made from time to time in such things as bumper styles, chrome ornaments, upholstery, and other matters that have nothing to do with how well the engine works or the wheels turn.

By the time those ancient insects got caught in the amber pitch of prehistoric pine trees, many types of insects were already stabilized and are still in style today. Among the beetles thus accidentally saved for our enlightenment were fireflies. Can you see one of the slim unlucky fellows with his feet in "gum-stickum," flashing his light more as the distress flare of a downed aviator than as the message of love it was designed to convey? Poor little machine-plus. He had delivered himself to an antique museum to be carefully preserved, out of commission for all time. If only he could have "left his lights on," what a priceless pendant the drop of pitch enclosing him would have become, amber glowing from within itself, outdoing diamonds!

Insects continually deliver themselves short distances on foot or wing, arriving at long journeys' end little by little. But in past ages they spread throughout the world in mighty migratory movements too, flying great distances in enormous numbers. Some still do. There are butterflies that ship themselves, under their own power, from north to south and back in annual migrations, somewhat like birds. Locusts set out on tremendous trips seeking food for their increasing swarms. Dragonflies at times, and several kinds of beetles in vast whirring throngs, fly far.

Sometimes long flights are accidental and take insects, through no effort of their own, to far-distant destinations. Many small light species are carried high aloft in rising currents of air and transported hundreds of miles. They are fortunate if the winds let them down on land instead of the open sea.

There have been hitchhikers about as long as there have been insects. At first, perhaps, the small kinds rode on the bigger kinds. But later on insects began hitching rides on the hair and hides of much larger animals, which made many extended journeys in the past from continent to continent or to islands, whenever the rising of land masses above sea

43

level connected them and made it possible.

No doubt insects are still riding far in this fashion on mammals and birds. And they get themselves delivered by carriers other than creatures, stowing away among the burdens of caravans overland and in the cargoes of ships and planes overseas.

Even the tiny, wingless, newly hatched larvae of some beetles hitchhike. They wait in flowers for a mason bee. Unnoticed by the bee, busy getting nectar, they climb aboard and, holding fast to one of the hairs on its fur, are airborne to its nest where, for weeks, they dine uninvited on bee's eggs, grubs, and honey. Only when it's time for them to pupate and become grown beetles do they stop feasting — an outrage on the bee, but for the beetles it is just a neatly-worked-out program for economical production and easy distribution.

Now let us take a close look at certain kinds or species of beetles in particular: "good" beetles, "bad" beetles, partly good or partly bad, or neither — just "indifferent" but interesting beetles. What are some of the many methods they have devised for success in life? How are they alike? How do they differ?

Part Two

LIFE HISTORIES

Here is the place to explain about the "jawbreaker" names that all our subjects bear. So many different kinds or species of plants and animals are living in this world (some hardly differing from related kinds) that an international naming and classifying system had to be established and used in all countries to keep the study of natural history from getting hopelessly mixed up.

Nearly a million different kinds of insects are known to science, with assuredly many more to be listed as discovered. And of these kinds, more than a third are beetles. Before the universal system was invented, some insects already had a common or "popular" name, some had several in use in various places, a number of kinds might share the same nickname, while many had no name at all, a condition causing great confusion.

But now with each known species given its official name and classified according to the system and with each newly found kind receiving a name not quite like any other, we can keep things fairly straight. The official jawbreakers are always in Greek or Latin, so that no matter in what language a book or scientific paper is published, students of all nationalities will know and use the same scientific name for any plant or animal they may wish to look up and read or write about.

To find individual labels for so many different kinds of insects, science has had to separate them into groups; first very large general groups, then dividing these groups into smaller, more particular groups, ever more minutely. Most of the time we need only to use the names of the last two groups to which a creature belongs, the group called its *genus* and a smaller division of that group called its *species*.

A list of beetles reads very much as do our own names in a telephone directory: our group or surname printed first, followed by our special given names or initials. The beetle's special name, the specific name, that is the name of the species, is always written with a small initial, even if it is already the name of someone whom the scientist describing the new species wishes to honor or the name of the state where it was discovered. As a further identification, the scientist then adds his own name, abbreviated, unless already very short. For example:

The great American entomologist, Leconte, describing two different species in the same genus of Ground Beetles, called them *Philotecnus ruficollis* Lec. and *Philotecnus nigricollis* Lec. We cannot always be sure just what a scientist has had in mind when giving a descriptive name to an unfamiliar creature. These two names seem to mean the "red-necked (*ruficollis*) child lover" and the "black-necked (*nigricollis*) child lover," both "as described by Leconte." *Philotecnus* names the genus, *ruficollis* and *nigricollis* name the two species, and "Lec." names the describing scientist. "Tecnus" means "child" and "philo" means "loving," and since these two species are grub and caterpillar hunters, "tecnus" must refer to the larvae (the children) of other insects that these red-necked and black-necked "philos" love (to eat, that is) in the same sense that one of us may "love" chocolate eclairs. If Leconte had wanted to honor a friend named Crabshaw, he could have called one of these beetles *"P. crabshawi* Lec."* He might have named either species *"P. californicus* Lec."* (the Californian child lover, described by Leconte), for California is where both of them were found, back in 1859. Since then, after further study, other entomologists have concluded that these beetles do not belong to the Old World genus of *Philotecnus* after all. So they turned the syllables around and

46

gave them a new generic name — *Tecnophilus* — which still means "child lover." It was also decided that *ruficollis* and *nigricollis* are not separate species, but merely varieties of one species, which has been designated *"croceicollis* Mén.," a name that also refers to a richly red-orange collar or neck. The present name of *ruficollis* is therefore *Tecnophilus croceicollis ruficollis,* and *nigricollis* is also used to show that it too is only a color variety of *T. croceicollis* Mén.

Things like this sometimes make it difficult to find certain species in a modern insect directory under names by which we have previously known them.

Nevertheless, let us now look up some "good" beetles. Let us begin with the Scarab (scientific name *Scarabaeus sacer* Linn.), the sacred beetle, so adored thousands of years ago by the people of ancient Egypt. They set it apart as a splendid religious object. Yet its work in the world, which classifies it as "good" today, is of a most humble kind. Though always immaculate itself, it is and may have been for millions of years, since the days of dinosaurs, a scavenger, a cleaner-up of unsanitary substances.

The people of Egypt didn't know its entire life history, and they misunderstood what they could see of it. Wherever horses, donkeys, sheep, cows, or camels had left what now is known as "barnyard fertilizer," there were bound to be scarab beetles busily making it into balls, rolling it away and burying it elsewhere.

One of the most intelligent persons of olden Egypt was the Empress Cleopatra, a woman of much charm, who could converse in seven different languages. Yet, no doubt, along with others of her day, she saw in the scarab's ball a symbol of the

47

Scarabaeus sacer (also called Ateuchus sacer or A. pius) with a food ball. L.S.

Tecnophilus croceicollis ruficollis Lec.

Pressure applied here and here

egg

grub full-grown & ready to pupate

The Ball

The "Pear" in section

sun, of Ra, their god most high, especially if the ball were being rolled from east to west, as the sun, itself a great ball, travels. And when a beetle rose from within the earth, where it had buried itself with its ball to feed on it in safety some weeks before, she thought she saw in its "rising from the grave," a resurrection, a symbol of immortality, of life forever defeating death.

Some of the old Egyptian notions still persist. Today in some books on insects, you can find mistakes regarding not only what was long ago believed, what the dung ball stood for and why, but also regarding the retelling as true of that old error about there being a scarab's egg in every ball. The fact is that there never is an egg in any rolling ball. To every scarab, male or female, the ball is simply a supply of provisions to be taken underground out of the sun's great heat (and the danger to themselves of being eaten by baboons, birds, or lizards), where they or their grubs-to-be can feed in peace and privacy.

You never see the baseball-sized dung ball that is provided for every grub-to-be's exclusive use. It is formed right where it is needed, in the nursery chamber underground, made from the materials of several smaller balls you may have seen being rolled to the burrow entrance and taken below by the beetle mother-to-be. There in the dark she shreds the stuff and shapes it all into a bigger sphere, entirely by her sense of touch. She couldn't model it more perfectly round were she able to stand off and size up her work now and then, whereas actually there is no light and not much more room in this insect sculptress's studio than for herself and her special kind of clay.

With the ball finished, she is not done. Pressing evenly all around the upper face of the ball, she forces that area to rise, taking more and more the form of the neck on a pear. As the neck is steadily extended by continuing pressure, its sides rise faster than its central part so that when the pear shape is completed, there is a little hollow at the neck's end where a real pear's stem would be anchored. In this little hollow the mother beetle lays a tiny cylindrical egg. She rakes together a mat of vegetable fibres (undigested by the grazing animal that unwittingly furnished the materials) and covers

49

the very end, concealing the egg but not shutting off its air supply. Then she leaves to start a new pantry-nursery for another grub child somewhere else.

Besides the several small dung balls she rolls away for her own provisions, the female scarab may collect enough more in separate burrows to make half a dozen bigger balls, which she also presses into "pears," leaving one egg in each. A grub, hatched from the egg, eats deeply into its supplies, hollowing out the inside of the pear and taking up the increasing room as it grows. Finally it falls into a mummy-like pupal sleep sometime in August. The pear's outer crust may have dried very hard, but with any luck, by the time the new scarab is ready to rasp its way out and go up to the surface of the soil to begin life as a feasting, ball-rolling beetle, the first fall rains will have drenched the land, softening and weakening its chamber walls; and here it comes, out and up into the brilliant sunshine, ready for a life of hard work and feasting.

In our present-day United States, certain ball-rolling beetles related to the sacred scarabs are often called Tumblebugs because they take so many spills in their progress overland. Instead of pushing a ball ahead of them or pulling it behind them, they push it backward, as do the scarabs, never able to see where they are going. The female beetle takes tumbles enough working alone. But often she is aided by her mate or has the unasked assistance of some highjacker scarab. Either of these will get on the ball's other side and pull, also backward. So into every dip and rut, and over every hump and bump, they trundle the treasure.

The mate really may be trying to help her, but the high-jacker aims to steal the ball when she gets busy digging a hole to hide it in. Yes, even among the "good" scarabs there are a few bad actors too lazy to build a ball for themselves, preferring to live by the work of others. But regardless of who buries the treasure, it does get distributed over the land and into the soil, thus enriching the fields, cleaning up the earth's much abused surface, improving the view, and clearing the air.

On his crop lands the farmer spreads whatever fertilizer collects outside the barn and plows it under, with good harvests in mind. He has no time to go all over his pasture taking up what the cows have left here and there, spreading it evenly about and spading it under. But most willingly, his Dung Beetle friends, relatives of the ancient scarabs, still perform that chore to serve their own purposes.

See how instinct outdid intelligence, how the humble insect stumbled upon the uses of a ball ages before thinking man discovered wheels! Millions of years before the Egyptians were rumbling to their destinations in carts and chariots, and thousands of years more before modern farmers ever crossed the crop lands with mechanized manure-spreaders, dung beetles were artfully forming perfect spheres and rolling their burdens to places of their choice. And because they still have only instinct to guide them, every untaught beetle of this kind knows the art and makes a perfect ball the first time it tries, whereas a human wheelwright must learn the trade, the apprentice improving only with time and teaching.

WHEEL & BALL

♂ pulling

♀ pushing

TUMBLEBUGS (U.S.A.)
Canthon laevis c. ⅔ L.S.

Fanciful thoughts of the Egyptians once elevated these insects, lowly refuse removers, to a place among the immortal gods. But a fact, unknown to the ancients, still sets them and various kinds of scavenger beetles high above most other insects. They have developed true family life, a status not all the "higher" animals achieve. Ants and bees, which we admire, raise their young ones with care and efficiency; yet there isn't a family of mother, father, and children. The ants' father is always absent. He mated with their queen-mother, high in the sky, when she was only a winged princess and he was a winged prince. But when they came down to earth, she took off her wings and went to work founding her city nation, while he crawled away somewhere and starved to death. The fathers of bees are drones, which loaf about the hive and do no work. They are finally driven from the hive by the busy workers, likewise to starve.

We have said that most kinds of insects don't live long enough to see, let alone to know or care for, their own children because their adult lives are very short compared to the time they spend as larvae. With most beetles it is enough to be a feasting larva for a long time and, after pupating, to mate, lay a lot of eggs — if the beetle is a female — near a good food supply for the hatchlings, flit about briefly, and die. "Safety in numbers" is their method, for besides placing a multitude of eggs near the proper food for their special kind of grubs, the beetles take no other measures to insure a new generation's growing up to keep their species alive in a world of enemies.

The scavenger beetles are somewhat different. The mother beetle may have much help from the father in digging an underground shelter where their children can grow more safely. And instead of laying one big batch of eggs and dying soon after, a dung beetle may live a full three years, laying only a few eggs each June but taking such good care of them that all will live and grow up completely before venturing forth in the dangerous world. Thus father, mother, and their children of various ages may rub elbows (or knock each other's knees) any early autumn day where barnyard beasts have left their peculiar kind of beetle's picnic or where a caravan has passed. The dung-beetle population is large, partly because individuals live so long and partly because they are so careful with their little broods of young ones.

Take, for example, a somewhat smaller kind common in Mediterranean countries, now called the Spanish *Copris* (*Copris hispanus* Linn.). The old-time Egyptians reverenced it only a little less than their sacred scarab. They might even have set it above the sacred one had they known how faithfully the mother *Copris* works to raise her family. Her mate works hard too (most unusual for male insects). They do not roll balls, but directly under the droppings of a long-standing sheep or goat, the male helps the female dig a burrow about eight inches deep and, at the bottom, a room a little bigger than a baseball but with a flat floor.

His job is to tote away all the soil she loosens. The armor on the back of his thorax seems designed especially for this purpose. With its rims raised on both sides and a high hump on its rear half, the thorax forms a very good hod for heaving earth up the burrow shaft. It serves somewhat like the hods of old-fashioned laborers who carried bricks and mortar up ladders to masons on high scaffolds. Both beetles, male and

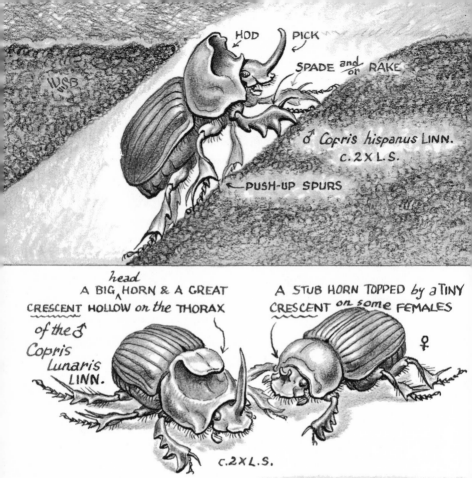

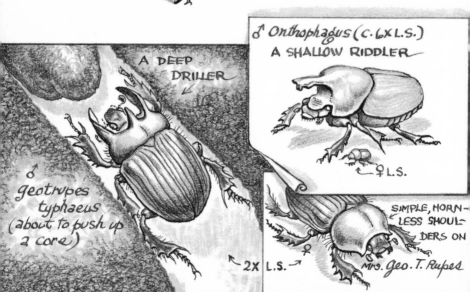

female, have a wide-based horn on the forehead, which may be useful as a pick in digging dirt.

When the tunneling is done, the husband helps his wife bring down provisions for the children who will grow and prosper in this place they have made. With their broad and jagged forelegs, they rake together many "armsful" of sheep manure and back down the shaft with it. In the room below she presses it all together, forming it neatly into a patty about the size of a small round bun. After that they rest a few days in their own little hideout. But when this "honeymoon" is over, he makes himself scarce, for now she has her special work to do and can manage better from here on without him.

She cuts off a portion of the patty, using the sharp forward edge of her face, called her clypeus, and the saw-toothed edges of her forelegs. Then, using her hindlegs also, she presses the piece into a perfect sphere about as big as a ping-pong ball. She makes a little depression in the upper face of this ball, lays one egg in it, and rakes in the rim of the depression loosely over the egg, thus tucking her baby in the egg to sleep till hatching time. She cuts another piece from the patty, forms another ball, and lays another egg in that. If there is enough material to shape up four balls, she will lay four eggs, her total output for that whole year.

But when they are laid, each in its own round share of the provisions, the mother doesn't climb up the shaft to feed herself and fly about, fancy free. She stands guard over the nursery and touches not a crumb of the food apportioned to her children. Now and then she goes carefully over the forms she has built, finding and destroying any mold that may grow on them, nipping off any tiny plants that sprout from seeds, feeling for and filling cracks that develop in the hot, dry summer, and remaining ever ready to kill blood-sucking ticks or to drive away various enemy insects that may come in looking for fat grubs to eat.

Day and night, for three long summer months she keeps watch over her little flock, eating absolutely nothing. She waits there in the dark until the first rains of September soften the crusts of the drying balls through which the children must cut their way. Sometimes she presses her head against a ball as though listening or perhaps only feeling the vibrations set up by the youngster inside it, trying to rasp his way out. By now all four children may have grown as grubs, passed through their mysterious pupal state, and become young adults, quite ready to come forth, although as yet no rain has arrived to free them.

In this situation they can be heard scraping away at the wall of what was their cradle but has now become a prison. Once they do break through, with or without the helpful rain, they wait in the nursery about two weeks while their armor hardens and deepens in color. Then, with their mother, they all go up to the light and freedom of the outside world, to fly and feast, carrying on their usual trade till the chill of winter drives them underground again to sleep till spring.

By May they are up once more and pairing with others of their kind. Their mother probably doesn't know one from another anymore nor even recognize them as her children. But her instinctive mother love lasted long enough to bring them up until ready and able to care for themselves and have children of their own.

Perhaps the prize for faithfulness should go to a still smaller kind of beetle called the Moon or Lunary *Copris* — *Copris lunaris* Linn. — because of the crescent moon-shaped hollow on the male's shoulders and the short crescent-tipped forehead horn on some of the females. Their family life is even more complete. The father helps the mother beetle with the digging and provisioning, but he doesn't go away when egg laying begins. He stays on patrol with his wife the whole summer long, likewise eating nothing. With safety thus made doubly safe, they are able to raise twice as many children as the Spanish *Copris* can. This is feasible too because they always set up housekeeping under a cow "platter," a much more plentiful source of supply than that left by a sheep or goat, as well as a bigger and better roof.

Wherever opportunities are good, we are almost sure to have other people about whose plans and methods interfere with our own. This is true for beetles also. As often happens, the *Copris's* roof may rapidly be riddled with holes made by the much smaller *Onthophagus* (dung eater) beetles. Yet beetles of this genus rate as "good" with humans because, though they may accidentally bother other "good" kinds of beetles, they also help to clear away unpleasantness. Not that they bury much. Each of their nursery chambers is only about two inches deep and half filled with a thimbleful of food for the grub. But these little fellows bore tunnels all through the platter itself so that it dries and breaks up more quickly, to be blown away at last as "heifer dust."

Better drillers and fillers of holes are the Geotrupid (earth borer) Beetles. Working at night, they dig straight down for a foot or more, under a heap of "road apples" left by a tethered horse or mule, then pack their diggings three-fourths full of the stuff. They bury much more than they can possibly use, sometimes all of forty cubic inches a night in one hole.

But instead of feeding repeatedly on what they work so hard to gather, the mated pair goes out again, seeking new places that need attention and doing the same work over every nice night all summer long. They make no ball at all, but though only half the size of the sacred scarab or the *Copris* beetles, they put more underground than either of them.

Geotrupes are the geologists of the insect world, always boring in and bringing up samples from lower layers of the earth. In the fall, some species sink a shaft all of three feet deep to reach a level less likely to freeze or dry out. The male brings up real "cores" — damply solid cylindrical samples of earth the female is mining far below. He always leaves the last core in the entrance to conceal it while he goes down for another plug to take its place. Around the rim of the thorax many males of the great scarab family bear various lumps and bumps, which, rising higher in some species, become horns. The thorax itself tends to be flattened on its forward area, even slightly concave, and together these features form a fine earth-moving mechanism.

When Mrs. Geotrupe has dug down far enough — a three to four foot shaft — she lays an egg at the bottom, and her husband goes out to find food for the grub-to-be. He brings back hard, dry sheep or rabbit pellets, holding them against his head with his forelegs and walking backward with the other four. He has as accident-filled a time of it as the tumblebugs rolling their ball, but at last he tumbles down his own home hole. He shreds each pellet with his jaws and sawtoothed forelegs, dropping the bits down to his wife, who packs them snugly into the burrow except for a little space kept clear all about the egg. She tops this pantry with a little earth and, above it, digs half a dozen chambers branching from the main shaft, laying an egg in each. With her husband's help she stocks every chamber in turn with shredded sheep or rabbit pellets, making sure that each hatching grub is well provided for.

The male geotrupe must get very tired pushing up all those damp cores from the deepening tunnel, the trips growing longer and longer. The task means almost a month of hard work. Now, if he takes it a little easier bringing in the pellets, who can blame him? Yet if he dawdles, the female makes a little squeak by rubbing the first joint of one leg against her abdomen. If he doesn't hear or heed her call, up she goes and gives him a good clawing. Even though he is passing the time in a crowd of his fellows, all as like him as peas in a pod, she will pick him out and "deliver the message." So he gets back on the job; but when it is all done, he is all "done in." Worn out, he crawls away, never to return.

The poor old fellow, if he was overworked, at least he was preferred by his mate to all others. She stays on watch below until the grubs have pupated and become new adults — imagos or imagines as they are often called. They go up and out of there together. And thanks to the hard work of their parents, the new generation is ready to carry on the race and trade of the beneficial geotrupes.

There seems to be some connection between following the toilsome trade of scavenger and being a good parent — among beetles, that is. To have a family, one must live longer and work more than is usual in the insect world. To carry responsibilities and to care for others require more energy and alertness than simply to supply one's own needs. Perhaps it is no accident that the kinds of beetles that have developed family life live as adults far longer than those that have not. And it may be that since they put so much into life, they also find it more meaningful and thus get more out of living.

There are a good many other kinds of dung beetles all over the world, similar in looks and habits to the ones we have been thinking about, all doing the same good work with varying methods. On the pampas of Argentina, a great cow country, earth-boring beetles lay the egg on top of, instead of under, the packed-in provisions. What a busy time beetles must have had in our Old West, keeping up with the roaming range cattle! And before the cattle came, when an Indian squaw gathered dry "buffalo chips" as fuel for lack of firewood on the lone prairie, she was raising the roof from many a beetle's underground wigwam. It wasn't only the Plains Indians who kept body and soul together by following the bison herds.

The farther into the tropics we go, the more astonishing horns we find on the heads and bodies of the scarab-like beetles and their relatives, their close or distant cousins. Some horns are plain and some are fancy, and many might serve as tools if not so overlarge as to be more hindering than helpful. Or they may be only ornamental, though probably quite useless in that direction also, for it cannot be proved that the females are either charmed or impressed.

Most of all, their mighty spikes and spines suggest terrible weapons. Yet when rivals fight, they only bump and push and wrestle a bit, trying to turn each other over but never biting, and almost nobody ever gets hurt. While the male beetles battle over her, a female beetle is likely to steal away, not caring a jot who wins or loses.

Golofa BEETLE SNAGGED ON A CREEPER BY HIS OWN 3-POINTED HOOK — VAIN ORNAMENT MAKING VAIN PURSUIT. *Golofa claviger*
×South America×
L.S.
(*Life-size*)

If they can't work more or fight better or charm the females more completely, their fancy horns must only be a burden and a bother to the males. Then why do they have them? What good are they? What are they for? Well now, everything in Nature is not "for" something. What good is a goat's beard or the tufted tip of a lion's tail? Surely successful

HERCULES BEETLES (*Dynastes hercules* L.)
A BATTLE IS LOST AND WON.
MALES ARE ABOUT 6 INCHES LONG.
× Central America & West Indies ×

lives could be lived without them. These features seem to have been added as if by Nature's doodling rather than by serious design.

If long, long ago a simple scarab type of beetle crept out of his pupal case with a hump on his back and a spike on his head, the like of which his kind had never had before, the new shape either would help or hinder him, or not make too much difference one way or the other. He still could find a mate, and many of the male beetles that hatched from her eggs would develop a pick and hodlike thorax just like his. Such a sudden change from what has been the normal character of a creature kind is not considered a monstrosity. It is called a mutation. Through it, these male beetles could become more helpful husbands, working with their wives all the more usefully because of this newly acquired equipment.

So a new and fancier species would become established and do very well in the world, right alongside the older, simpler

kind. But later on, in some members of the new species, the tendency to grow and sprout even bigger horns, humps, and ridges, might be redoubled and a still newer species be created by more mutations, producing such exaggerated tools that the males could no longer get into the tunnels to help the females dig even if they cared to. This newest overbuilt species would have to survive — if possible — in spite of, not because of, its peculiarities. The males might be able to invent a few new tricks in sparring for the females. But the hornless females, still retaining the original basic design of the race, would have to do all the work of raising families themselves. If the males continued growing ever more grotesque and clumsy, so that they even failed in fathering new broods, that kind of beetle would quickly die away.

It seems to be a rule that the bigger the beetle, the more extravagant the armor. Another rule in Nature is that overgrown creatures with oversized armaments are on their way to becoming extinct. This principle has applied even to the ways of human beings. The knights of old carried ever heftier swords, wore heavier and heavier armor, and had to straddle the saddle on bigger and bigger horses till steeds and riders could hardly carry their burdens. The developing use of gunpowder, almost mercifully, put an end to such overgrown devices.

There once were giant deer with antlers big enough to amaze a moose, overheavily and fancily tusked elephants, monster cats with fangs so long that they got in the way, and many others afflicted with too much of various good things. Nature scrapped all these designs. But long before such mammals lived and died out, many kinds of reptiles had gotten so overly large that no amount of muscle could support their weight. Some dinosaurs had always to wade belly-deep, buoyed up by the water. The outlandish armor developed by others was of a style surprisingly like that worn by some of the sacred beetle's relatives today.

But history doesn't always repeat itself. With all rules there are exceptions, said to prove them. And one thing that may save the overbuilt beetles from going "the way of all flesh" is the fact already mentioned, that the females still stick to sensible styles and sizes and, with or without help from the males, take very good care of their children.

Although not related to the scarabs, other scavengers, called Sexton or Burying Beetles, will hide underground the dead body of any animal not too large for them to manage. A bird, a snake or frog, a mouse or chipmunk, a rat, or sometimes even a great old groundhog, they will attempt to bury. Within half an hour after a creature dies, some of these big beetles

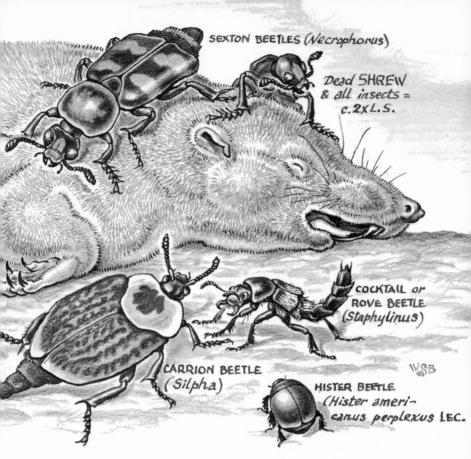

SEXTON BEETLES (*Necrophorus*)

Dead SHREW
& all insects =
c. 2 × L.S.

COCKTAIL or
ROVE BEETLE
(*Staphylinus*)

CARRION BEETLE
(*Silpha*)

HISTER BEETLE
(*Hister ameri-
canus perplexus* LEC.

WSB

may arrive, too gaily dressed perhaps for their profession — in black to be sure, but with bright orange patches across their coattails.

Suppose a pair of them has scented death with their very keen antennae and flown from who knows how far away. They have come, ready to dispose of the body. They climb and walk about on it as though sizing it up. Will it provide enough food for a whole family until the children are ready to be graduated at pupating time? They crawl under it, testing whether the earth where it lies is soft enough and free of rocks. If the answer is "yes" to both questions, they commence digging, pushing soil out on all sides from underneath the little corpse. A ridge of loose particles rises around it like the ripples in water that form about an object falling in. As more and more soil is moved from under it, the body sinks, seeming to shiver, resting as it does on the heaving backs of the husky, hard-working beetles.

When it sags below ground level, the diggers begin to form a chamber, cutting the side walls of the crypt more carefully. At about the same time, the ridge or ripple of loosened earth piled all about, starts sliding in and little by little covers the body, more slowly but very much as water closes over a sinking stone. If the sextons encounter tough grass roots, they cut them with their mandibles and go on digging. They don't have to think that the roots must be cut before the corpse can be lowered any farther. Nature has given them the shears and the inclination to use them wherever such problems develop.

A scientist, watching a pair at work, tied the tail of their dead mouse to a stake by a string, so that the latter end of the little corpse would not sink as they dug beneath it. He was not teasing but testing their intelligence by giving them an unusual problem. They were puzzled at first but finally found the string, cut it, and gave the mouse a "proper burial." Before they are through, the original pair may be joined by several more sextons, all eager to work, and the obstructions are quickly removed.

Before digging at all, if, on inspection, the ground where the body lies has been judged unworkably hard or stony, the beetles scout around for a better site not too far away, three or four feet distant perhaps. Here and there they dig test holes, and when a better place is found, the big job of moving the body begins. No attempt is made to push, pull, or roll it. But now, instead of going under it with their backs uppermost, the beetles turn over and slip under with their legs up, their claws hooking among the fur or feathers. Facing toward the chosen place, they push up under the body with all their legs, inclining them forward while extending their telescoped abdomens, the tips pressed firmly against the ground. The dead thing seems almost to come alive. Moved by unseen forces, it rises slightly and slips forward a fraction of an inch at a time. When it is finally where they want it, the burying beetles dig it under in the usual way. Once it is out of sight, all but two of the diggers depart, leaving only one pair, a male and a female, in possession. How it is decided who must go and who may stay is hard to say. The first pair to arrive could have done the whole job unaided, though it would have been slower and more fatiguing. By rights, the prize is theirs, and perhaps it really is "finders keepers," no matter who helps them, however much.

There is a great deal more to be done. The beetles have worked hard and steadily, it being always necessary to get the burying done before the carcass is carried off by a carrion crow or buzzard or eaten by the quick-hatching maggot children of flies. But now the sextons can take a break, long enough to help themselves to the maggots (thus helping us humans in our endless war against the flies) a feast in which they are almost sure to be joined by rapacious Rove Beetles, those slim, bloodthirsty weasels of the beetle world. If flat-bodied Carrion Beetles come to feed on the dead mouse or bird, they can be knocked aside by the busy buriers. They won't follow the feast very far into the earth.

Having secured the body underground, the sextons now presumably embalm it in some way as yet unknown to science. It does not decay but remains in a pasty gray condition, preserved food for themselves and their family-to-be. As a nursery for the latter, they dig a hallway leading off from their pantryful of provisions. Along this corridor they hollow out little niches wherein the female lays her dozen or so of eggs. Meanwhile, the hairs or feathers of the dead creature have come loose, and the two beetles collect all that inedible material out of the way at one end of the pantry. When the grubs hatch, they creep along the hallway to the pantry, whereupon their mother pours some of her dissolving saliva over a portion of the preserved food, partly digesting it where it lies and making it semifluid. She sucks up some of this slurry and feeds it, mouth to mouth, to her babies until they are big enough to help themselves directly.

If the provisions last about two weeks, it will be long enough, for then feasting and fattening and growing time is over and pupating begins. The mother and father leave now, to seek new burying tasks, while the grubs creep off alone and bury themselves, their very own first burying job. In little cells in the soil they pass through the mystery of the complete making over — the pupal stage — and, at the end of about ten days, there is a general "coming-out party." They emerge from their cells transformed, reborn as young adults, ready to go out and undertake great undertakings, following the family trade of helping to keep the world we live in as sanitary as Nature ever inclines to have it.

There are other beetle claimants for honors as "public

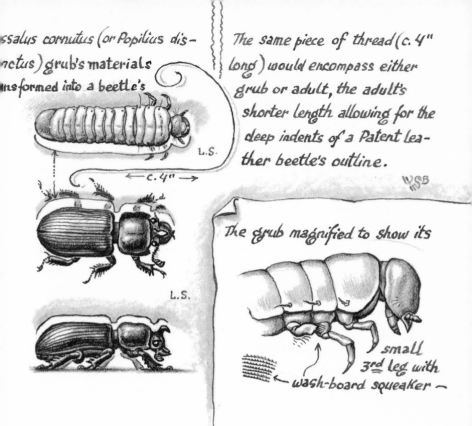

...ssalus cornutus (or Popilius dis-
...nctus) grub's materials
...nsformed into a beetle's

L.S.

← c. 4" →

The same piece of thread (c. 4"
long) would encompass either
grub or adult, the adult's
shorter length allowing for the
deep indents of a Patent leather beetle's outline.

L.S.

The grub magnified to show its

small
3rd leg with
← wash-board squeaker —

benefactors and best parents" among insects. These are not
exactly scavengers but beetles that nevertheless do help improve the soil's condition wherever old trees fall or younger
ones are cut by man and wastefully left where they lie. Inside
such tree trunks and their stumps, after they have begun to
rot and soften with moisture, these beetles are likely to set
up housekeeping.

They have a variety of common names. Bess Bug is one
(nobody knows why). But they are Horn Bugs and Peg Bugs
clearly because of the short horn that rises and then points
forward on the heads of male and female, a very handy hook
for anyone who wants to tie a beetle to a toy truck and see

how much it can haul. *Passalus cornutus* Fab., meaning "peg-horned," has been their Latin name for years, but recently for some obscure reason the official name has been changed to *Popilius disjunctus* Illiger, in case you wish to look these fellows up in a beetle directory.

In some localities another common name for them is Patent Leather Beetles because of the smooth lacquered look of their jet-black covering. Bess, peg, horn, patent leather beetles are big, about one and a half inches long. If you should take a hatchet and open a rotting stump, you might find their galleries cut all through the touchwood, the part that, through decay, has already softened into punk. They have made these galleries or tunnels in feeding themselves on the damp, decayed material and partly to create a dwelling for the family where, with their parents, all the children — grubs big and little, older and younger — may freely move about, two or three generations together.

The two rear legs of a *Passalus* grub are very short and shaped more like the paws of a dog than the feet of a beetle grub. Like a dog scratching fleas, it scrapes one of these hard-pointed paws across some corrugated chitin on the first joint of the leg ahead of it to make a raspy little squeak. At this signal, the mother or father beetle will come and feed it by unswallowing some of the touchwood they have eaten and predigested for the tender stomachs of their infants. The adults squeak by rubbing wing covers and abdomen together. Thus all members of the family can keep track of each other in their dark dwelling place.

If your chopping hasn't opened the stump too much, the grubs will continue to live in it, eating the rotted portions

Stag beetles (*Lucanus elaphus* Fab.) L.S.
Southern U.S.A.—*They cannot kill each
other.*

♀

♂s

nd in parts of
rope it is un-
wful for any-
ne else to kill
hem.

WSB

and growing big and fat, over two inches long, bigger than their parents.

They will reduce during their pupal stage, the stuff they are made of being re-used to fashion them into more compact, more complicated heavily armored animals. The miraculous change comes only after three or four long "grubby" years, but they step forth at last, splendid in patent leather, the height of their own fashion.

By that time their home will be no better than a tumbledown shack, decayed, eaten, and digested; nothing now but a heap of nourishment for a new tree there or for a blueberry bush or luxurious ferns. Near another rotting stump you might find adult Stag Beetles, *Lucanus,* or, inside it, the big grubs eating, eating, and like their patent leather cousins, helping to reduce dead wood to fertile soil.

71

In the northeastern United States you will meet *Lucanus dama* Fab. (Latin for "shining stag"), and in our southern states it will be *Lucanus elaphus* Fab. (Latin plus Greek, also for "shining stag"). *L. dama* Fab. is about one and a half inches long, and *L. elaphus* Fab. is three inches, over one third of its length being the "antlers" of the male. His outsized jaws, with extra points projecting, do greatly resemble the antlers of a buck deer. Yet no one could fail to see that they are jaws and not horns or antlers at all. The fairly simple Latin name of *Lucanus dama* Fab. has now been changed to a really stunning jawbreaker, *Pseudolucanus capreolus* Linn.

Because of his jaws *Lucanus* looks extremely dangerous, literally "armed to the teeth." So it is surprising to find that he can't bite hard enough to puncture the skin of your finger, though his grip is by no means pleasant. Try cutting a piece of cardboard with the tip ends of some long shears. You can't exert much power. But using the other end of the blades, close to the pivot and handles, you can cut very well. It is the same with the jaws of *Lucanus;* they are too long for good leverage.

Rival males, fighting for a female, can't bite hard enough even to dent each other's armor, whereas the lady herself, with short "normal" jaws like nail-clipping nippers, can bite hard. So can the grubs that hatch from eggs she lays in the earth around the rotten stump. They eat their way into the stump with no trouble at all. But their heavily armed father, having left his own grubhood home, for all his great jaws can never bite his way back in again.

Formerly, in England, perhaps because no one knew just what, if anything, he could do with his pincers, people believed *Lucanus* would set a house afire by carrying red hot coals from the fireplace to the straw thatched roof. It would be as foolish to think today that he could be trained to bring ice cubes in his tongs for one's toddy. Actually, instead of attacking and eating other insects as he looks so able to do, he only flies to where he smells sap seeping from a break in an oak tree's bark and sips it up till satisfied.

In temperate climates *Passalus* and *Lucanus* are "good" beetles. Vegetarians, dining on what is left of dead trees and drinking a little sap from the live ones, they do us some service and tax us very lightly for it. But most vegetarian beetles are "bad" in our lists. They eat or spoil our food in field, garden, store, and warehouse. Many kinds eat the wood, bark, and leaves of living trees, while others damage the dry wood in lumberyards, houses, furniture, and tools. They destroy much and cost us a great deal year after year.

Some species (the Scolytids) are small indeed and some other kinds quite large. Females of the smaller kinds, eating under the bark of living trees, lay eggs in the tunnels they make. The grubs, hatching, eat in a fanwise pattern of tunnels, spreading out on both sides away from the mother's tunnel so as not to interfere with each other. If enough of them get to work between the bark and wood, the tree's sap can no longer flow and it dies, or a disease, unwittingly brought in by the beetles, kills it. The Fir Engraver (Bark) Beetle and its grubs cut a family pattern that is a portrait of the very tree they are destroying as it will look when they get through, its trunk and every branch, with all the needles dropped away in death, and the whole tree already fallen.

Instead of feeding just under the bark, other species of

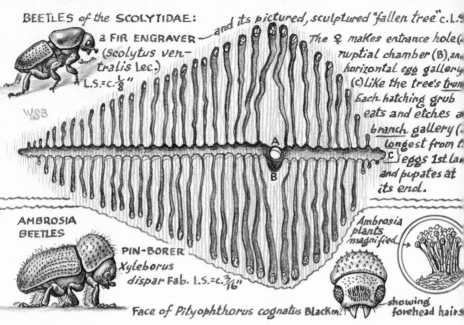

BEETLES of the SCOLYTIDAE:

a FIR ENGRAVER — *and its pictured, sculptured "fallen tree" c.L.S.*
(*Scolytus ven-
tralis* Lec.)
L.S.=c.⅛"

WSB

The ♀ makes entrance hole(A,
nuptial chamber (B), and
horizontal egg gallery
(C) like the tree's trunk.
Each hatching grub
eats and etches a
branch gallery (longest from t[he]
C eggs 1st laid
and pupates at
its end.

AMBROSIA
BEETLES

PIN-BORER
*Xyleborus
dispar* Fab. L.S.=c.³⁄₁₆"

Face of *Pityophthorus cognatus* Blackm.

Ambrosia
plants
magnified →

showing
forehead hairs

wood-spoiling beetles bore deeply into the sapwood, even
into the heartwood. These, the Ambrosia Beetles, are especially interesting. The female bores her way into the tree or
fresh-cut log, turning like a tiny gimlet and making a round
tunnel just big enough to let her pass. She bites out widen-
ings now and then (niches for turning around) and one
bigger than the rest as a room for herself and her mate. He
helps by pushing all her jaw dust (it looks like sawdust) back
along the tunnel and out of the tree. These beetles do not eat
the wood they cut. They live on a special kind of fungus
called ambrosia.

In a tuft of hairs on her head, the female brings along a
supply of the fungus spores, like minute seeds, and plants
them on little beds she makes of jaw dust here and there
along the damp passage she is boring. They will grow quickly
and, spreading, provide ample food for all. When some of the
ambrosia is eaten, it grows up again and again, like asparagus.

Funguses (fungi) are related to mushrooms. And just as we have edible mushrooms and poisonous kinds, so these beetles have to know the difference between their ambrosia fungus and other kinds that could make them deathly ill. Carefully they keep the latter weeded out, good insect gardeners that they are.

There are two kinds of ambrosia beetles. In one kind the female cuts short branch tunnels, called cradles, along the sides of the main gallery and lays one egg in each. She closes each little cave with a mass of ambrosia fungus. The babies hatch and eat the food so handily placed for them. If one eats its way clear through and out into the main gallery, the mother beetle clears away the rubbish and tucks the baby in again with fresh supplies. She gives constant close attention to all the cradles, a very good nurse in a lively maternity ward.

The other kind simply lays eggs at intervals along the main gallery, and the hatching babies creep about eating ambrosia tips wherever they find a patch. They are free to join their parents and the other children in a widened part of the gallery that serves as a sort of living room for all. Here, then, are two more kinds of beetles that have a true family life, father and mother bringing up the children together. Not only that, they plant and cultivate their own food, something few creatures below mankind can do, a distinction shared only with some species of ants and termites. And they entomb their dead. If one of them dies, the body is sealed off in a special niche, thus possibly preventing sickness from spreading all through the family.

Yet remarkable and honorable though they are in these

respects, ambrosia beetles rate as "bad" from our point of view, for besides ambrosia fungus, various tree-killing and lumber-spoiling fungi frequently ride on beetles into wood, sometimes destroying forests like a plague, killing off all of one kind of tree or another across great sections of country. We have lost our chestnuts. We are losing our elms.

Of the bigger wood-loving beetles that make bigger holes and tunnels in trees as well as in cut wood, many are classified as Longhorns or Longicorns because of their very lengthy feelers. Some are called Capricorns (goat horns), their great curving antennae, even their faces, being most suggestive of the big wild Ibex goats of Old World mountains. Frequently longhorn species are named for the kind of tree or plant they infest, as the round-headed apple tree borer, the oak longhorn, the maple borer, the locust (tree) borer, and the red milkweed beetle.

They are beautiful streamlined beetles, many species being marked by handsome patterns or pretty colors. So are the "Metallic Wood Borers," which are not longhorns but Buprestids whose larvae are termed "flat-headed borers," as distinguished from the longhorn larvae or round-headed borers. Both these big kinds of borers are widespread through the world, and, as with many other insects, the warmer the climate, the bigger they come. The bigger the beetles, the bigger the trees they attack. Sometimes when a great tree is felled and made into furniture, a grub, unseen, remains alive inside the wood. In the hot, humid tropical forest it might have been ready to pupate in about two years. But in the cut lumber, shipped to a factory in a cooler country, the grub's progress is greatly slowed down. If it survives a period in the

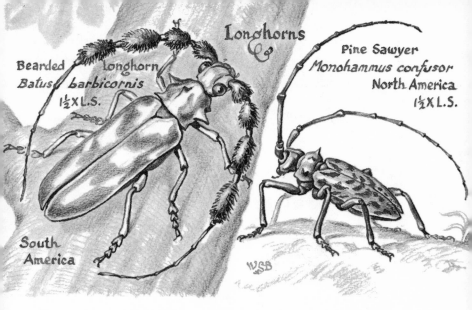

Longhorns

Bearded Longhorn
Batus barbicornis
1½ X L.S.

Pine Sawyer
Monohammus confusor
North America
1½ X L.S.

South
America

WSB

drying house, inside a heavy length of timber destined to be fashioned into furniture, it may live on ten to twenty years in parts cut for a big desk or other massive pieces before eating its wooden way to within a sixteenth of an inch of the polished surface to pupate.

Can you see the scene at a stylish musicale, where the hostess takes a peculiar pride in her perfectly modern piano, which she has had built in the hippopotamus-heavy style of old-time "square" pianos to harmonize with all her antique furniture? In his grand finale the famous visiting musician strikes the keys in a crashing crescendo, and out from high on one of the instrument's rhinoceros-like legs pops the forward end of a big beetle, staring, opening its awful jaws, and waving long quivering antennae at the horrified ladies seated nearest the instrument. Amidst the applause, the bowing performer mistakes their "Oh! Oh!'s" for gasps of appreciation.

But a distinguished entomologist, who long has wanted a specimen of this exotic species, happens to be present. It is

L.S.

The long endurin
larva

2XL.S.

Splendid Buprestids
("Flat-headed Borers" or
"Metallic Gem Beetles")

his moment of triumph more than the musician's. Holding the insect aloft, its legs all a-wiggle, he tries to calm the audience (though far from calm himself) and announces for the edification of all, "We have here a splendid insect, *Buprestis splendens,* a metallic wood borer, which while still a grub and while the piano leg was only a part of a tall jungle tree, must have entered the wood of this piano — at least ten years ago. Similar cases have occurred from time to time in other furniture made from tropical timber." Then wrapping the buprestid in many folds and turns of his big silk handkerchief, he bids his hostess good night and hurries home.

You must be wondering how beetle grubs can live and grow and become adults with nothing at all for food and drink at any time but wood, especially those that dwell for years in the bone-dry cut wood used in furniture and house building. Beetle larvae living on this dry diet are as moist and fat and juicy as any free-roaming, dewy leaf-eating cater-pillar. How can this be? Why don't they shrivel up and die soon after hatching?

This is a commoner condition in creatures than is generally realized. It is possible for certain beetles to live on bone-dry food and never drink so much as one drop of dew because of metabolic water, which is produced within themselves simply by their breathing air and digesting their food. Chemical changes, taking place in their metabolism, supply all the water they need. This process also takes place in the breathing and digestion of other kinds of animals, especially in the reptiles and mammals that live in waterless deserts. With mammals such as cows or human beings, not enough water is manu-factured in their metabolism; and they lose so much besides that they must drink more water to make up the difference and supply all their body's needs.

With a beetle grub it is the other way around. It produces so much metabolic water and loses so little that it never needs to drink at all. As it breathes, a little vapor is lost through the spiracles, but a greater amount of moisture is made right in the body. Reached by the inhaled oxygen, slowly some of the beetle grub's fat is oxidized, chemically "burned," pro-ducing the poisonous carbonic acid gas (referred to in System IV: air intake — an insect's breathing), which is exhaled, plus water, which is retained for the body's use. Fat is composed of carbon, hydrogen, and oxygen atoms, arranged together in a certain definite way. In this slow "burning" process the atoms get separated and rearranged. Some of the hydrogen atoms combine with oxygen atoms in the ratio of two to one. This is H_2O, the metabolic water.

The same thing happens when beetles or their grubs eat wood, though the process involves a preparatory step. Damp, rotted wood eaten by beetles like *Passalus* and *Lucanus* has already been made digestible by bacteria and fungi working in it. But beetles that eat unrotted wood must bring their own bacteria to table to ferment the tough wood, to "rot" it right in their own interiors, for wood is largely cellulose, an entirely indigestible compound of atoms. This structure of atoms, six of carbon, ten of hydrogen, and five of oxygen ($C_6H_{10}O_5$), has to be broken down and rebuilt to form digestible starch and sugar. But fine chewing and good digestive juices alone cannot do this for a wood-eating beetle. Without help it would fill up on its favorite food only to die of thirst and starvation.

Other kinds of beetles that live on moist foods will still drink water or sap. But fortunately, for a non-drinking, dry-wood-eating beetle, there are living in its gut millions of microscopic animals — protozoans, or micro-plants known as bacteria; these cause the swallowed wood bits to ferment in such a way that the cellulose atoms get rearranged, forming the necessary starch and sugar. The micro-creatures and their beetle host are then able to share the freed nourishment. All unknowingly the beetle may also digest some of its so helpful passengers, thus obtaining the proteins and vitamins needed to balance its diet. Remember the Walrus and the Carpenter who invited the oysters to supper and then ate them all? Well, anyway, when food is being digested, whether wood or oysters, some hydrogen atoms get combined with oxygen atoms, two to one, forming still more metabolic water.

Yet, though the dry-wood eater has enough moisture, the precious supply must always be conserved. A screen of hairs in each spiracle catches some of the vapor that would otherwise be exhaled. A beetle doesn't perspire, and very little skin is exposed to the drying air at joints in the armor. The armor itself is covered with a waterproofing wax. A beetle doesn't urinate, almost all the water being reabsorbed by the body before the uric acid is expelled as a solid salt.

There really are relatively few "bad" kinds of beetles when we consider the two to three hundred thousand other kinds that never do us any harm. Yet even so, the troubles these few can make are so numerous that it sometimes seems as though all kinds must be bothersome. Take what happened to our entomologist, for example, right after his triumph at the piano recital. In spite of all he knew about beetles, they got the better of him. He hurried home to the little old house in the woods where he worked and lived all alone. He popped his prize beetle into a killing bottle and then, happy but weary, went to bed. Besides being crazy about "bugs," he was, like his hostess, very fond of antiques and had bought an old four-poster bed at an auction a few days earlier.

Unable to rest, he lay listening to a most disquieting sound coming from inside the bedpost nearest his head.

"That is either *Xylobiops basillaris* Say or *Anobium punctatum* DeGeer," he thought. And well he knew that the grubs of either *Xylobiops*, the Shot-Hole Borer, or *Anobium*, the

81

Common Furniture Beetle, could chew the inside of the bedpost to powder without its showing on the outside at all. The rasping jaws of the hungry grubs crunched on. The entomologist turned over and lay closer to the wall. But now he heard another sharper sound, an intermittent tapping behind the plaster close to his ear, answered by more tapping farther up. He knew the sounds were made by adult Deathwatch Beetles of another *Anobium* species, long supposed by superstitious people, in any house where they were heard, to be ticking off the time until someone should die. Of course, he knew this wasn't so, that the beetles, by whacking their heads against their hard wood tunnels, were simply telegraphing "love calls" to locate each other. Their many grubs would soon be eating in the uprights. Trying to think more cheerfully, he remembered his big buprestid borer, but soon was saddened to recall that the grubs of various large longhorns might even then be weakening the heavy ceiling beams and floor of his old house. The Old House Borer might well be one of these.

"A plague on you, *Hylotrupes bajulus!*" he muttered and was answered by a loud "crack!" in the beam above him. Then a bedpost at the foot sank through the floor and jarred the gnawed post near his head so that it broke off, strewing powdered wood and beetle grubs on the carpet. He leaped out of bed and switched on the light. If he tried to live there any longer, the deathwatch beetles would be right after all. He would die there. To move in the small hours of the morning seemed absurd; yet he often had heard these sounds before, warning him that he would have to get out sooner or later. He had bought the house too hurriedly without making sure it was sound.

"Sound!" he thought. "It's full of sounds and sawdust! So must my head have been!" He thought he'd need breakfast to strengthen him for the job of moving, so long postponed. But when he went to make some biscuits, he found the flour full of Flour Beetles and their many meal-worm children.

"Ten times ten *Tenebrios!* I'm being eaten out of house and home!" Growing calmer, he told himself there really wasn't time for cooking. He decided to put on old clothes for the dusty work of toting all his books and papers and his trays of insects — collected and mounted over the years — out to the little truck he hadn't used for many months. But when he took his heavy work shoes from the closet, he found that little beetles had been feasting on the leather.

"Dermestes, Dermestes! You are the derndest pest-es!" It helped to joke when things weren't going well. But his heart sank when he recalled where else these tiny scavengers might be. They make a meal on anything that once was part of an animal, getting into lard and bacon and preserved meat of all kinds, chewing holes in anything made of wool — rugs and carpets, felt hats and fleece-lined slippers — and all articles of natural silk. They clean up what bigger scavengers have left, living high on dried bones and gristle and skin, eating hair, fur, and feathers. They can spoil a coonskin cap and winter underwear as completely as moths will do it. Nothing is too large or too small to interest them. They will ruin a mounted giraffe in a museum, but being so small, they will also crawl through very slight cracks and eat the dry insides and joint-connecting membranes of every mounted insect in a specimen case, causing them to fall apart, unless care is taken to prevent it.

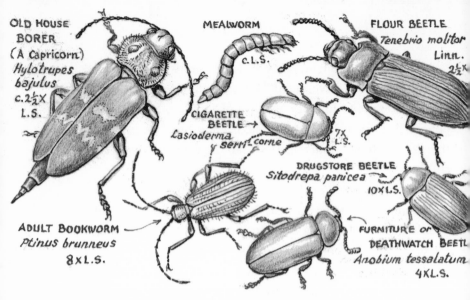

OLD HOUSE
BORER
(A Capricorn)
*Hylotrupes
bajulus*
c.2½X
L.S.

MEALWORM

c.L.S.

FLOUR BEETLE
Tenebrio molitor
Linn.
2½X

CIGARETTE
BEETLE →
*Lasioderma
y serricorne*

7X
L.S.

DRUGSTORE BEETLE
Sitodrepa panicea
10XL.S.

ADULT BOOKWORM —
Ptinus brunneus
8XL.S.

FURNITURE or
DEATHWATCH BEETL
Anobium tessalatum
4XL.S.

Scientists should never be careless. Yet they can be as absent-minded as the rest of us; and alas, so busy had our entomologist been with other matters, he had not remembered to renew the pest repellent in his specimen cabinet for ever so long. By now the mounted insects in many of the drawers were in a sorry state, and so was he. He turned to his shelves but found that bookworms, the tiny grubs of Ptinid Beetles (using dry pages for food) had tunneled straight through volume after volume, starting at one end of a shelf and only turning around to eat their way back at the other. He could hardly bear any more but had no time to waste feeling sorry for himself.

Suddenly the ceiling over his bed, on the other side of the room, crashed down and crushed the four-poster. Then the electric lights went out. He had just picked up his precious buprestid and, with only this of all his possessions, he stumbled toward the door. It wouldn't open. The eaten-out frame was resting on it. He tried to open a window. It wouldn't

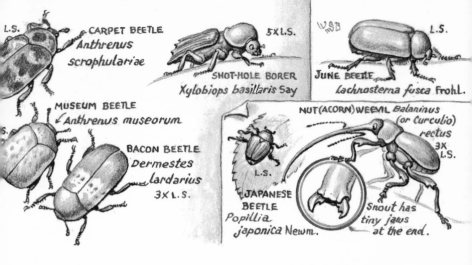

L.S. CARPET BEETLE
*Anthrenus
scrophulariae*

5X L.S.
WSB
L.S.

SHOT-HOLE BORER
Xylobiops basillaris Say

JUNE BEETLE
Lachnosterna fusca Frohl.

MUSEUM BEETLE
Anthrenus museorum

S.

BACON BEETLE
*Dermestes
lardarius*
3X L.S.

NUT (ACORN) WEEVIL *Balaninus*
(or *Curculio*)
rectus
3X
L.S.

L.S.

JAPANESE
BEETLE
*Popillia
japonica* Newm.

Snout has
tiny jaws
at the end.

slide; the frame was warped. Awful cracking sounds kept coming from splintering timbers, and, now really scared, he smashed the window and scrambled out just as the whole house collapsed. A short circuit in the broken wiring set the kindling wood remains afire.

"A good fumigating," he thought. "A little late but better late than never." Then he shrugged, got into the truck, and in beetle-eaten bathrobe and slippers drove toward town to get the fire engines. "Got to take this philosophically," he told himself. "After all, I am a Ph.D.," and he smiled like his ancient hero, good old Socrates.

For once he had had all he needed of "bad" beetles — and so have we, almost. Not that there aren't others as troublesome: the kinds that eat tobacco in warehouses, the ones that can live on medicines and poisons in drugstores, even digesting strong insecticides with no difficulty, and of course other pests in our lawns, gardens, shrubbery, and trees, like the Colorado Potato Beetle, the Japanese beetle, and the May and June "bugs" we see so often, not to overlook the evils of weevils, those elephant-nosed beetles that do so many kinds of damage. But we don't need to study them here. The United States Department of Agriculture, your State Agricultural Experiment Station, and entomologists in and out of natural history museums have studied "bad" insects long and carefully, since, as a nation, we must know all we can about our enemies in order to defend ourselves successfully.

Because "friendly" insects do us no harm, we tend to neglect them. But a great many books and leaflets have been published about "bad" beetles, usually illustrated with drawings and photographs. The United States Department of Agriculture also offers "picture sheets" in full color, showing eggs, larvae, pupae, and adult beetles of many species on the plants they attack, with their life histories printed on the other side. These book-size color prints and many of the leaflets and bulletins cost only a nickel apiece.

It might be a good idea to paste papers and pamphlets like the above into a loose-leaf notebook, along with notices and articles about beetles you find in magazines and newspapers, to make a fine beetle reference book of your own. Write to the Superintendent of Documents, Washington 25, D.C., and ask for a price list of everything they have on beetles (Coleoptera) so that you can make a selection, and then send an order with a check or money order payable to the Superintendent of Documents.

If you'd like to start your own first-rate museum collection of beetles, ask the Superintendent also for the booklet, "Collection and Preservation of Insects" — Miscellaneous Publication No. 601, U.S. Dept. of Agriculture. It costs only 20¢ but is very good and helpful for beginners. A price list, labeled PL 41 "Insects," costs nothing. Ask for the latest edition.

You don't need to enclose postage when you write to a Government agency if you live in the United States (taxes take care of that), but when asking a museum or a busy individual scientist for help or advice, put in a stamp for the reply. Say please and thank you and write your name and address clearly. Good manners oil the wheels. A more painstaking answer will reach you all the sooner.

You could write to the Smithsonian Institution, United States National Museum, also at Washington 25, D.C., and to your State Museum and State University for price lists of their publications on beetles and other insects as well. Publications have a way of going out of print. Then you can only see copies in libraries, if they have them, and you can't take them home to study or paste into your book. So see what several sources have for sale.

Of course, the entomologists have studied "good" insects that help us by eating the "bad" ones. Such are the little Ladybugs or Ladybird Beetles, whose children — contrary to the old rhyme — need no protective care, being fierce and bloodthirsty larvae, able to pounce on their prey successfully, yet not liable to be preyed upon by other creatures.

The name ladybird beetle is better than ladybug, for whereas all bugs are insects, not all insects are bugs by any means. Bugs are jawless insects that have a sharp hollow bill for sucking blood or plant juices. No beetles are bugs, whatever their popular names, for all beetles (even the nearly needle-nosed weevils) have jaws to eat with. No bugs are beetles, but some of them are beetle food.

Aphids are small bugs that suck the sap of our garden plants and sicken our flowers, often spreading diseases from plant to plant. They have relatives called Mealy Bugs that raise havoc in greenhouses, and others called Scale Insects, which can so infest an orchard of oranges or other citrus fruit as not only to ruin the crops, but also to kill the very trees. Ladybirds are avid aphid eaters both as larvae and adult beetles, each consuming about 600 aphids in a lifetime.

In the late fall millions of these tiny beasts of prey gather on (of all places) the tops of mountains, where they crawl under fallen pine needles, dead leaves, and litter on the forest floor, huddling together to wait out the cold weather. The agriculture departments and insectaries of several states and the nation can collect them easily then and, keeping them in coolers, are ready in the spring to ship them to any farmer who needs a large number turned loose in his infested orchard or grain fields.

It isn't always necessary to telephone your government for help. On the continent of Europe, when there is an aphid plague in the British Isles, "the word gets around" among the ladybirds in some unknown way. Spurred into action by this "intelligence," a ladybird army of millions, paratroopers all, has flown across the English Channel several times in remembered history and saved the day for England. Many beetle fliers have fallen into the sea and been washed up "dead as herrings" in windrows along the shores, but these casualties never prevented the rest from accomplishing their mission. How did they know there was a job to do, a picnic to be had? Did the west wind bring the news? Could the beetles actually smell the sweet aphids across twenty miles and more of water?

A few ladybirds failing to fly away to high places for the winter are likely to waken early in the spring before you see other beetles of any kind. Leaving the cracks around your window frames where they have sheltered through the colder months, they are baffled by the glass that shows them the outdoors but prevents their reaching it. Kindly let your friends out. They may not fly to heaven, turn into angels, and reserve a place for you there, as some people still assert, but just having them alive on earth, close by, will help insure healthy, beautiful trees and shrubbery for your neighborhood — and better gardens.

Open the window and guide them gently out. They only want to find a breakfast of eggs laid on various plants by other kinds of insects. They will feed on these until aphids reappear and start sucking sap again. Ladybirds are hardy little beetles. Although nights still are frosty cold, they don't go back to winter quarters but just crouch in the crotch of two twigs and wait for the rising sun to thaw them out for further feeding on insect eggs.

There are many species of ladybirds with various designs of dots on their backs. Of them all, four thousand kinds deserve our annual vote of thanks for their helpfulness. But in so large a family there are bound to be a few "black sheep." Several species here and abroad are vegetarians that spoil some of our food. We have, in the United States, *Epilachna borealis* Fabricius that attacks pumpkins, squashes, and melons. And we are pestered by *Epilachna varivestis* Muls. (or *E. corrupta* Muls.), the Mexican Bean Beetle that eats the leaves and stems of bean plants. Grubs of the latter never

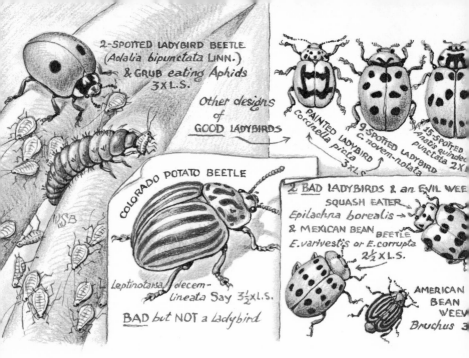

2-SPOTTED LADYBIRD BEETLE
(Adalia bipunctata LINN.)
& GRUB eating Aphids
3 X L.S.

Other designs
of
GOOD LADYBIRDS

PAINTED LADYBIRD
Coccinella picta
3 X L.S.

9-SPOTTED LADYBIRD
C. novem-notata

15-SPOTTED
Anatis quindeci-
punctata 2 X L.S.

COLORADO POTATO BEETLE

Leptinotarsa decem-
lineata Say 3½ X L.S.

BAD but NOT a ladybird

2 BAD LADYBIRDS & an EVIL WEE
SQUASH EATER
Epilachna borealis →
& MEXICAN BEAN BEETLE
E. varivestis or E. corrupta
2½ X L.S.

AMERICAN
BEAN
WEEV
Bruchus 3

gnaw through the pods to get into the bean seeds themselves, leaving that to another kind of beetle altogether, the American Bean Weevil, *Bruchus rufimanus* Boh. Save for a few vegetarians, exceptions to the rule, the legion of ladybirds is all on our side in mankind's world struggle to produce enough good food for everyone.

Although it is so important to us, the work of these little beetles is fairly easy for them and safe to do. After all, aphids are perfect pushovers. They are weak, wet, sweet, and tender, the easiest sort of prey for ladybirds. But we have other carnivorous beetle friends that attack more powerful and better armed insects, equally injurious to our provisions and supplies as aphids and other bugs. These friends are the ground beetles, hunters clothed in dark metallic-looking armor, belonging to a very large family called Carabidae.

The idea of "idae" (id-ee) at the end of an insect's scientific title is to name its family, a bigger group to which the creature belongs, bigger than its genus and species. Well, this family of beetles, the Carabidae, contains many genera (plural of genus) and many species that are commonly found during the day, resting under stones and other objects on the ground. They usually set out on their hunting trips after sunset. If you are a garden spader, some kinds may be turned up from fairly deep diggings.

A few species of ground beetles are vegetarians, herbivores, which, because of their tastes, may damage our growing plants at times. But the great majority are wide-ranging hunters, attacking whatever small creatures they can overcome. The well-armed and armored grubs are as fierce as the grownups. All have medium large, extremely strong, sharp-biting jaws. Words in your dictionary always used to describe them, besides "carnivorous" (meat-eating), are "ferocious" (cruelly savage), "predacious" (preying, plundering), and "voracious" (always hungry). They kill and eat a great many root-ruining grubs as well as the grownups of various kinds of beetles, June bugs and Japanese beetles among them. They feast on many other insect pests in the garden, cutworms included, plus the slugs and snails that nightly gnaw holes in lettuce and the like. Their appetites are never satisfied; so from our point of view they are helpful; they are "good."

One quite common carnivorous but rather small, rather pretty ground beetle has a deceivingly less ferocious appearance than its relatives. Its wing covers are dark blue-black, and the rest of it is all light orange-tan. It has a delicate look, but it can take care of itself. Its method has earned it the bold-sounding name of Bombardier. This is because, if molested, it can instantly become at will a piece of mobile field artillery. Its legs are the wheels, and its rear end is the telescopically operated protrusile retractile cannon.

In the firing chamber just within this gun, glands secrete certain acids and gases, which, coming together, explode with an audible "pop!" and vaporize behind the beetle like a tiny puff of blue smoke. The gun then recoils but can quickly resume firing position if one shot is not enough. The smoke can burn your finger, making a red, angry spot, which turns brown and dry and smells horrid. Nobody has explained how a creature of flesh and living tissues can contain and secrete such caustic chemicals without being burned itself. But it can and it does, sometimes shooting about six rounds in succession if need be; and birds learn to leave the little bombardier alone.

Especially "good" and good-looking are the big *Calosoma* ground beetles. Calosoma means "beautiful-bodied," referring to their bright metallic colors. We can only wonder why Nature has clothed so many of the Carabidae in drab black or dark brown but favors *Calosoma scrutator* Fab. (Beautiful Searcher) with a blue head and legs, blue or violet thorax with golden trim, and green wing covers edged in scarlet. In this gorgeous costume he steps onto a stage above his station, playing the role of tree climber, high above his earthbound fellow species, seeking incessantly aloft for caterpillars that damage our forests.

Even while still only a grub, *C. scrutator* Fab. will get into the fold of forest tent caterpillars and act like a wolf among sheep or a weasel in a henhouse, only more so. If two scrutators happen to enter the same tent full of caterpillars, between them they clean out the lot. Then the bigger grub may eat the smaller one for dessert. They are voracious to the point of being occasionally cannibals.

Calosoma sycophanta Linn., blue of head and thorax, with green wing covers but without scarlet trim, was imported from Europe to help gobble up the gypsy and brown-tail moth caterpillars, which also are ruinous to our trees if left unchecked. It is said that he too will drop in for lunch at an ugly tent caterpillar colony and stay until refreshments give out.

Another member of this genus, *C. calida* or *C. calidum* Fab., confines his caterpillar hunting to our gardens and meadows, where he specializes in the cutworm and cankerworm kinds. *Calidum* means "hot," and he is generally called the Fiery Hunter, a very good and helpful fellow who, though not as colorfully clothed as the other two, is impressive in his own fashion. He is so black that he looks purple, and his eyes are a blazing copper color. So are several rows of dents all down his wing covers.

Fully as beautiful as the most colorful *Calosomas* are the Cicindelidae (sissindelidee), cousins of the Carabidae, but hunters by day, which reflect the light so brilliantly that their nickname is Sparklers. The sun never sets on the flashing cicindelids; they are found all over the world. Like the cars all made by one manufacturer, they come in a variety of models and metallic colors. They are more commonly called tiger beetles, a reference not to their coloring but to their natures, being, if possible, even more predacious than the ground beetles. So predacious are they that one kind actually

93

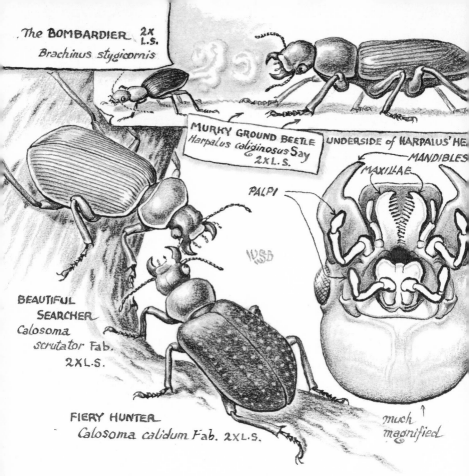

The BOMBARDIER 2X L.S.
Brachinus stygicornis

MURKY GROUND BEETLE
Harpalus caliginosus Say
2X L.S.

UNDERSIDE of HARPALUS' HEAD

MANDIBLES

MAXILLAE

PALPI

WSB

BEAUTIFUL SEARCHER
Calosoma scrutator Fab.
2X L.S.

FIERY HUNTER
Calosoma calidum Fab. 2X L.S.

much magnified

follows the ebbing sea, hunting for beach-fleas between the tides.

Unlike their carabid cousins, many of whose eyes are none too good, tiger beetles out in the blazing sun have especially well-developed eyes and are extremely quick, light fliers, very hard to catch. One of them, resting a moment in a favorite spot on an unpaved path where you walk, will fly up and land a few yards ahead of you, waiting till you get close again, only to take off over and over as though playing a game. Finally up he goes and, circling widely, returns to the precise place where you first disturbed him. To us it looks like a teasing joke, but to him it is just good tactics for safety's sake.

As a grub, the tiger beetle is an ugly duckling. Of all beetle larvae, you would probably pick him out as least likely to grow up and transform into one of the world's most beautiful insects. This seemingly shapeless grub is a still-hunter, a watcher in ambush. He doesn't stalk and pounce on his prey, as he will when adult, but waits in the opening of his burrow for some unsuspecting insect to come close enough to be snatched in his jaws. Then he backs down the burrow, dragging his struggling victim to the bottom, where dinner is served.

Just in case the prey may prove strong enough to drag him from his hole and possibly escape, exposing him in turn to attack from enemies (birds especially), he has two sharp spurs on his back that he jabs into the burrow walls, grappling hooks, holdfasts for just such emergencies. If ever there is "complete metamorphosis" in the insect world, it occurs in the life of a tiger beetle. He changes from a lazy, drab stay-at-home, a rather repulsive-looking trapper, to an athletic, free-roaming, esthetically handsome hunter whose elegant form is all aglow from the gold reflecting through translucent green, blue, violet, red, and orange in the outer layers of his armor. Added to this coloring are pretty white or yellow markings that vary from species to species.

Although in this book we may not yet be through considering "bad" beetles, we are purposely paying more attention to the "good" ones and to those others so often overlooked, the "indifferent" or "neutral" kinds that are just as interesting as the bad ones, often more so. Incidentally, it might be fair to beetles in general to remind ourselves that all other insects can be divided into the same three categories — helpful, harmful, and neutral — and that "bad" beetles are by no means the only insect threats to our well-being.

There are beetles that rate "good" at one stage of their lives and "bad" at another. This may be so with some of the Water Beetles, which, when first hatched, could kill and eat mosquito wrigglers (to our benefit). But growing bigger and bolder, these fierce beetle larvae hunt ever larger creatures until their favorite game is tadpoles. Tadpoles, allowed to live, turn into "friendly" frogs and toads that feed on mosquitoes, flies, and other pests every day through many years of usefulness.

The tadpole killers are often called Water Tigers, but more truly they are vampire dragons that do all their dreadful deeds beneath the waters of what appears to be a placid pond. They get to be three inches long, and they swim about with great needle-sharp crescent-shaped jaws at the ready till, espying a tadpole, they sneak up and suddenly snatch hold of its soft belly. Like the fangs of a rattlesnake, the jaws are hollow hypodermic needles, and piercing the tadpole, they inject a paralyzing poison (which undoubtedly dulls the victim's pain), followed by a digestive fluid. The latter liquifies the tadpole's innards so that they can be sucked with the blood into the innards of the vampire beetle larva without its having to swallow any water while dining below the surface.

Sometimes the tables are turned. The dragon will one day have to creep ashore to pupate in the mud beside the pond. If a bullfrog (once a defenseless tadpole himself) happens to be sitting close by, he surely will stab the villain with his sticky tongue and swallow it whole. The dragon will become energy for the frog instead of becoming a big black Diving Beetle, *Dytiscus* by name. If it gets past the frog and "holes up" in the bank, it may yet be dug out and eaten by a musk-rat, shrew, or mole, or by some mud-probing, long-billed bird.

But every *Dytiscus* dragon that succeeds in pupating goes right back into the pond as a beetle, to resume attacking everything it can overpower, even including small fishes. Now it is more directly troublesome to man. You can imagine what havoc these beetles can make when several get into the rear-ing ponds of our fish hatcheries.

Another kind of big black water beetle, about an inch and one half long, is also a bloodthirsty dragon in its larval state. But after pupating, it reforms and only returns to the water to lead a useful and "blameless" life of scavenging. By some, the Water Scavenger is called the Great Black Water Beetle, by others, the Great Silver Water Beetle (depending on whether it is viewed from above or below), but labeled, in Latin, *Hydrophilus* (water-loving).

Transformed in tendencies as it is in physique, it hunts no more but, like a mild sheep, grazes on the minute algae that grow as a green lawn on the pond's bottom and on sta-tionary objects in the water. It will clean up any crumbs it comes upon, left from the feasts of other creatures, seeking shreds of meat still clinging to the chitinous skeleton of some luckless grasshopper that fell into the pond and was eaten by a swarm of little Whirligig Beetles. As in other matters, there are exceptions to the dietary rules of hydrophilids. Some species and individuals slip into their old ways now and

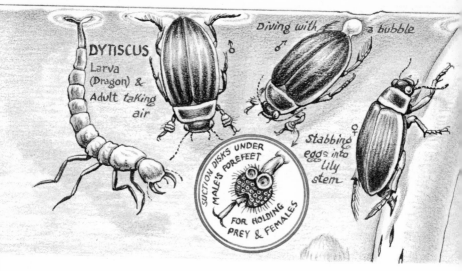

DYTISCUS Larva (Dragon) & Adult taking air

Diving with a bubble

Stabbing eggs into Lily stem

SUCTION DISKS UNDER MALE'S FORE FEET FOR HOLDING PREY & FEMALES

then, attacking other creatures, especially pond snails, for a meat dish.

Water scavenger beetles make good aquarium animals to watch. These are the ones that always seem to have shimmering silver bellies. The silver is really a close-fitting film of air, held in place by many little hairs on the insect's underside. This isn't all the air a silverbelly takes below on his submarine foraging. He has other reserves. His abdomen may be slightly rounded underneath, but on its upperside it is flattened somewhat like a ship's deck. The wing covers bulge up over this decklike area, making a protected watertight air chamber. His breathing holes or spiracles open in this chamber. They are located all along the margins of the deck like a ship's scuppers, though they conduct air in and out of the beetle instead of water overboard as from a vessel.

If you float a little block of weathered wood in the aquarium, your Madame Hydrophilid will adopt it as her retiring room. Obliged always to swim in order to stay below (the air she carries continually tending to raise her), she will welcome

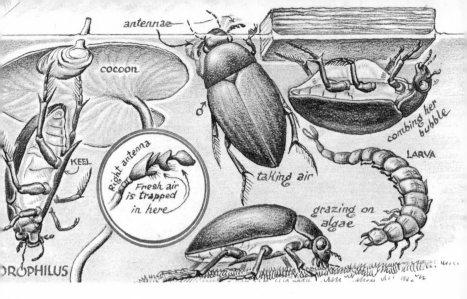

antennae

cocoon

♂

taking air

Right antenna
Fresh air is trapped in here

KEEL

combing her bubble

LARVA

grazing on algae

ᴅROPHILUS

the little raft as a place where she can remain submerged without kicking or clinging to anything. She will lie, back down, buoyed up by the water, her toes lightly touching the wood above her. Supported so handily underwater, she can do a leisurely job of washing, that is, scrubbing her head and body with her legs. Any other hydrophilid, male or female, would make similar use of this convenience.

Now watch your beetle closely. You may see her do a puzzling thing. She will open her wing covers ever so little and, with her hair-fringed hind feet, draw some of the reserve air (from the chamber just described) expertly around her rear end and onto the upturned underside of her belly, adding it to the air already there and making a great bulge where we usually see only a sort of flat "silver plating." This air, just transferred from back to belly, has been in and out of her tracheae a number of times. It is used air and needs refreshing by contact with the water. But exposing it thus, without losing any as free-rising bubbles, takes inborn skill. Now she does a still more curious thing. The fringes of hair on her hind and middle feet are there primarily to help her swim. But they are more than oars, for we see her use them as combs, bringing them across the big bubble that clings to her belly, warping it first with strokes from one side, then from the other. She is helping to rid it of carbonic acid gas and increase its oxygen content. But combing her bubble looks funny, reminding us of our absent-minded entomologist who once poured syrup on his head and scratched his pancakes.

Next she returns the refreshed air to the chamber under her wing covers, seeming, by opening them slightly, to create a vacuum there into which the big bubble slips without letting in any of the surrounding water. Exactly how she accomplishes this feat is one of the puzzles that may be solved some day by a sharp-eyed amateur observer. Whatever she does is not enough. Every now and again she must climb carefully up the side of the little raft and hold one or both of her club-shaped hairy antennae out of the water. Bringing them back, she scoops down a "feelerful" of air on each, increasing the silvery layer that covers her belly. At the same time she sucks some of that layer back under her wing covers, again by moving them bellows-style six or seven times and, probably by a barely noticeable expanding of her abdomen, fills her tracheae full of freshened air.

She doesn't go up to get more oxygen, as is generally supposed. She can get all the oxygen she needs by exposing her air supply to the enveloping water and combing it as described. But this also causes a great loss of nitrogen into the water. Air is about four parts nitrogen to one part oxygen. Nitrogen is a gas very necessary to a creature's health. When it dissolves away into the water, it must be replaced. By its loss into the water, the volume of the beetle's air supply keeps shrinking and must be built up by taking air at the surface. Of course, when Lady Hydrophilid rises for nitrogen, she collects some oxygen as well.

Sometimes she may put her whole head and part of her thorax out of water, as though trying to gather air more directly than by the feelerful. There is a big spiracle on each side of the thorax close to her head. These spiracles, surrounded by hairs, let air in but keep water out. If you are lucky, you may see your hydrophilid once in many trips to the surface, float on her back free of the raft, upturned belly all exposed, getting the most air with the least effort in the shortest possible time. This unusual occurrence is likely to take place on very humid days.

Besides an air layer on the belly, hydrophilids have a keel, a long, strong spine of chitin running like a ridge down the center of the thorax, very useful to beetles that swim with strokes first from one side then the other. A keel keeps these beetles on course, preventing them from veering with every alternate stroke. Dytiscids need no keel, for they thrust back with both hind feet at the same instant. They also get their air supply more simply and directly than hydrophilids do, putting the rear end out of water much as they did when larval vampire dragons. They do not have an air layer on the belly but collect air under their wing covers and may carry a spare bubble attached to the rear end during dives.

Why doesn't the spare break loose and rise to the surface? Well, just as water clings to things in the air ashore, air clings to things under water. Water clings to the hairs on a dog till

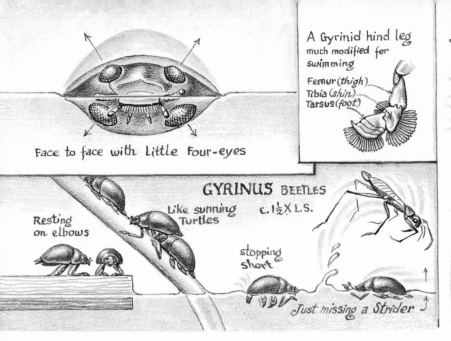

Face to face with Little Four-eyes

A Gyrinid hind leg much modified for swimming
Femur (*thigh*)
Tibia (*shin*)
Tarsus (*foot*)

GYRINUS BEETLES
Like sunning Turtles   c. 1½ × L.S.

Resting on elbows

stopping short

Just missing a Strider

he shakes himself; air clings to many minute hairs on the belly and feelers of hydrophilids, or to the fringe of hairs on the rear air syphon of dytiscids. At night both dytiscids and hydrophilids may breathe air directly as land beetles do, for they like to leave the water and fly about, frequently gathering at electric lights in town. But this is bad for them as many never get back to the ponds again.

In the ponds dytiscids are more direct than hydrophilids in other ways. A dytiscid female lays her one thousand eggs here and there on water plants with the least amount of trouble. Madame Hydrophilid spends about five hours carefully spinning a silken cocoon around a bubble to hold her mere 100 eggs "all in one basket." She finishes it off with an upraised air tube that reminds us of a periscope but is really a ventilator. She likes to attach a cocoon to the underside of a water lily leaf, but if it "slips its cable" and drifts on the pond, it is "a very good sea boat," unlikely to capsize even in a stiff breeze.

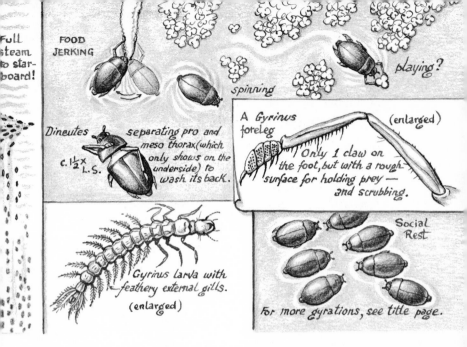

Full steam to starboard!

FOOD JERKING

spinning

playing?

Dineutes c. 1½ × L.S. separating pro and meso thorax (which only shows on the underside) to wash its back.

A Gyrinus foreleg (enlarged) Only 1 claw on the foot, but with a rough surface for holding prey — and scrubbing.

Gyrinus larva with feathery external gills. (enlarged)

Social Rest

For more gyrations, see title page.

Other species of dytiscids and hydrophilids are smaller than the ones we've been considering, living like miniatures of their great relatives. But the smaller water beetles, sure to be seen by anyone who strolls beside a pond or quiet stream, are the lively little whirligigs, ever swimming on the surface in dizzy spins and with sudden changes of direction. These gyrators are members of the Gyrinidae. They come in several sizes just as the ripe seeds of watermelons do. So close is their resemblance in size, shape, and color to watermelon seeds that in the old days it was seriously believed "water beetles come from watermelons."

Because they have been watched making fancy turns on the water by many people for many centuries, they have been called many things besides whirligigs, such as Writes-My-Name, Coffee Bugs, Scuttlebugs, and so forth. To one who has spent much time both at sea and beside still waters, they seem to have a good deal in common with dolphins and porpoises: their dark, shiny backs rounding out of the water as they move in lively numbers, great and small, but almost never without at least a few companions. And along with their sociability they appear to have the dolphin's quality of playfulness.

Now, the idea that any insect will really play, as the higher creatures do, is enough to raise the honest eyebrows of scientific students of animal behavior. But if we watch whirligigs a lot on the ponds and in a home aquarium, jotting down every move they make, our long list will include many actions impossible to interpret as anything but frolic. Play is prompted partly by an excess of energy with which the whirligigs are overwell supplied. Where they get so much vim, vigor, and vitality is a mystery when we see what a minute amount of food satisfies them for an entire day. But they do have this excess energy, and they use up a lot of it in ways that accomplish no more serious or important results than we humans do in water sports or in playing tag or dancing, or than dolphins do in their games.

Viewing these little beetles as machines-plus, we may see them as a flotilla of modern speed boats. Or they may suggest the first American "ironclads," the Merrimac of the South that fought the Monitor of the North to a draw one very long morning during our Civil War. Bulging above the waterline with sloping armored sides, they are Merrimacs all — Merry Macs indeed, playfully scampering about each other for no apparent reason except that they feel good and like good company, showing it in their endless gambols.

The scientific behaviorist might say that all this rushing about is only a feature of their social life, not play but life itself. Or it might be said that one whirligig circling a resting comrade several times, sideswiping it repeatedly in a series of figure eights, caroming off and finally running straight at the resting one full tilt to bump it awake, is only due to the attraction of the sexes.

However, there is no sex attraction between a whirligig and a tiny duckweed plant. Yet one of these beetles will swim, slalom-fashion, through a wide cluster of the floating water vegetables, finally selecting one and pushing it free from the rest. He will swim circles and figure eights about it, push it along some more, then suddenly abandon it for other sport. He doesn't eat the plant or anything on the plant, seeming to use it simply as a toy.

In millions of years and as many miles of gyrating around their friends and other objects, is it not possible that, among these insects, some elements of play may have developed? There are "higher animals" that don't know how to play even in their childhood (guinea pigs, for example), so why not a few lower animals that do know how? All the possibilities of character were present in the very first germs of life on this planet from which we all descend. In the lost and found department of natural history, some kinds of creatures developed certain traits while others evolved along different lines. If many have lost certain qualities, others may have found some very similar. Play may mean nothing to a guinea pig, but does that prevent a whirligig from enjoying a lively gambol with others of his kind?

One whirligig will collide with another on purpose, possibly to stir up some fun. But in spite of their furious speed and quick comings-about, they seldom, if ever, bump by accident. Like porpoises in the sea or bats in the air, they have a sonar signal system, sending out squeaks too tiny and high-pitched for our unaided ears that echo back to them from any object ahead, allowing them time to steer clear or stop before running into it. It is fun to know that these boat-like little beetles have sounding devices similar to those that keep great ships out of collisions and shallow waters. Whirligigs may detect "rocks ahead" by wave vibrations of the water itself, as well as by the sound-wave echoes of their own squeaking. When first placed in an aquarium, while they dash about madly, seeking a way of escape, they don't crash against the glass sides, seeming instead to sense the barrier, though unable to see it at all. Even having two sets of eyes doesn't help them in this.

They do have two sets or, more exactly, their two eyes are divided at the waterline, the high-beam halves looking for food or enemies from the air, the low-beam halves doing the same underwater. These are Nature's original bifocals, possessed by whirligig beetles ages before Ben Franklin invented similar aids for human eyes. Divided eyes are fine for creatures that spend their time "between the devil and the deep blue sea."

From the air the devil may appear in the form of a swooping swallow, not averse to catching whirligigs while scooping a drink on the wing. An unnoticed bittern, standing like a dead branch sticking out of water, may jab at the beetles if his fishing is not going too well. A small frog, sunning on a lily leaf, may shoot out his quick sticky tongue to pick one off the water, should the school swim near enough. Or ducks will be pleased to mix beetle meat with their duckweed greens.

From below, though the pond is not a deep blue sea, fish will rise to strike at insects on the surface. Salamanders, turtles, frogs, water snakes, muskrats, even crawfish, all are water beetle eaters on occasion. And in the deep South, any baby alligator will surface in the midst of a whirligig school, snapping rapidly left and right for a meal of half a dozen.

Of course the majority always seem to escape by artful dodging and unpredictable evolutions. If you are in a boat, reaching for a few with a net, a very few is what you'll get time after time, though you may sweep at a monster whirligig armada composed of thousands. They manage to stay just a mite beyond your reach, or dodge the net when close enough to be caught, if only they would stand still the fraction of a second.

Because of their constant quick turnings, you may read in the words of one naturalist that whirligigs have no sense of direction. But in such great gatherings of the little fellows we see convincing proof that this is not the case.

As your boat comes slowly toward a mighty school, all of them moving along without haste in the same direction, close together but with no one bumping anyone else, preserving an outward calm, though every watchful eye is on you (a strange and probably dangerous giant), suddenly somebody panics. He is either the most timid beetle on the near side of the fleet or a brilliant admiral. He puts on full steam and takes a sharp tack to starboard, crossing the bows of half the others in the whole armada. Those he crosses turn to follow at the same increased speed, and a rapidly widening wedge of them develops as all, in a spreading sequence, come about to follow the leader away from you. Beetles to the fore are soon swept into the new formation, and presently, in a mighty maneuver, precise as a drill often practiced, one thousand and one not-so-dizzy whirligigs are speeding on an undeviating course, all showing high ability to hold one definite direction as long and as far as is desirable.

What a formidable fleet it would be if all these Merrimacs were equipped like the bombardier beetles! Yet, though only chitinous clad and mounting no guns, it is said by some observers that they can defend themselves by discharging a milky fluid to cloud the water when obliged to turn submarine and dive. This is the old smoke-screen device used by squids and certain shrimps in the sea, behind which they can scurry to safe hiding places. Whirligigs seem disinclined to take a bubble and dive; the surface of the water is their world. They will dive only if dodging and speeding away can't keep them out of your net or some other danger, but they dive reluctantly.

Whirligigs will dive to avoid a serious threat from below as well as from above, living as they do in a habitat exposed in both directions. They are deathly afraid of fishes and find it safer to dive into a tangle of subsurface water weeds than frantically to try outswimming a hungry perch or bluegill. With their underwater eyes they may see the enemy approach, but they rely on his odor to warn them as well. If you hang a very small sliver of raw fish in your water-beetle aquarium, though they see no fish, they will instantly catch the scent and dive. Not for at least two hours, or for as long as you leave the terrifying tidbit in the water, will they rise and resume their habitual whirling.

One or two, being near the raft when they smell fish, will

crawl quickly onto it and get a good drying off while waiting for fancied danger to pass. An occasional drying off is good for them, but they prefer to get it under peaceful conditions, piling up together now and then like sun-bathing turtles. A whirligig drying off by himself will rest on the elbows of his long front legs and the tips of his short middle pair, with his rear legs tucked up beneath him. He looks like a boat overturned and laid on racks, his back being the boat's bottom. After his own bottom has aired a bit, he may slump down and rest like a land beetle.

As we have seen, a whirligig can swim in a beeline if he chooses, but he prefers curves. He changes direction very often, yes, but he hasn't lost his wits or his way. Continuous turning every which way is, in effect, a form of whirligig life insurance, always there whether danger is present or not. Even though a whirligig may not see its enemy in time to dodge, if, simply by habit, it makes a sudden turn every few paddle strokes, it is likely to elude the enemy anyway. A twisting target is hard to hit, whether we call it a whirligig, scuttlebug, gyrinid, or writes-my-name. Also with the swerving habit, the swimmer is less liable to stray in a straight course over deep open water, where hiding from a preying enemy is most difficult.

The "social whirl" of the gyrinids may be to their advantage in capturing their own prey also. To miss no opportunities, they circulate, surprise a mosquito wriggler up for air, find a floating meal of mosquito eggs that might be missed on an unswerving course. They don't just swim right past a lily leaf. They turn suddenly, speed toward and onto it. A whirligig may catch a dawdling fly or bug off guard this way, then drag it into the water, where as many fellow beetles as can will crowd around to help eat it. Or little writes-my-name may charge without warning at a Water Strider, one of those sucking bugs that skate on the surface, a rival hunter. The bugs may leap high and let the gyrinid pass harmlessly beneath, but sooner or later one of them will leap too late and be hauled back to the water to be eaten.

It may be difficult to believe that these charming, mischievous, innocent-looking little water beetles are fierce beasts of prey. But they are. They will kill and devour whatever other insects of the land or water they can overpower, alone like a dytiscid or swarming like a school of bloodthirsty piranha fish. Together they don't hesitate to tackle a great grasshopper kicking in the water or a floundering moth twenty times the size of one of them.

Whatever insect falls their prey, they always try first to reach its most defenseless region, the upper side of its abdomen just behind the thorax. This is an easy thing with moths and flies but a real struggle in the case of a land beetle, whose wing covers clamp tightly down and are very hard to pry under. They attack with savage fury, getting a grip with their jaws and pushing back with their long front legs, straightening first one, then the other, jerking themselves to left and right till a piece of their prey comes out.

The front legs are for climbing up plant stems or onto lily leaves and resting on elbows, as well as for dealing with the prey and cleaning up after a meal. They are folded into grooves under the thorax when the whirligig is swimming, so as not to spoil the streamlined speed in the least degree. Grooming is always done in the water. The front legs make short swift strokes, passing the combs on the front feet under the face and over the head. They are long enough to reach over the gyrinid's back and comb almost the whole length of the wing covers.

Members of another genus of bigger gyrinids, *Dineutes* by name, improve on this. The three sections of the thorax fit snugly together, but, by stretching, these *Dineutes* beetles are able to open a space between the first and second sections. Through this space they thrust their long front legs, reaching the entire surface of the wing covers. They make motions identical with ours when we wash our backs, first one arm then the other, or both at once quickly, like someone taking a shower in a great hurry. The middle legs seem to take no part in the clean-up, but the rear pair scrub the flat tip of the abdomen, which projects beyond the wing covers but can be bent down and reached by the rear legs.

Unlike the dytiscids and hydrophilids, whose middle and hind legs are long, somewhat flattened, and fringed with hairs as oars (for not very speedy progress), gyrinids have those legs fringed but very flat, short, and wide, each about the shape of one lengthwise half of a ship's propeller blade. Any two of them, making a half revolution apiece, achieve the same propulsive power one propeller blade of that size would have.

The strokes are so swift and the insect so small that we cannot catch the action clearly; we cannot tell in what planes and arcs and in what sequence the four swimmer-legs apply the power. A slow-motion movie would help a lot. Maybe one has been made by now. The navigation of these small machines-plus is so efficient and so effective that it might pay our naval engineers to study them, just as they learn from porpoises. Whirligigs can literally "turn on a dime," and not just turn, but spin like a top on their own axes.

It often seems that they spin like ballet dancers, simply as part of their choreography. But then again a very fast, tight watch-spring spin appears to be an expression of pleasure and excitement. If you provide pet whirligigs with a shred of chicken (cooked or raw), suspended at the aquarium water's surface, they will rally about; each will take a sniff at it and then swim around for a moment. Some may "fall to" immediately. But one or two, having smelled the delicious dinner, act as though ecstatic at the idea of eating it. Much as we might clap our hands, hug ourselves, and jump for joy at some delightful prospect, then spin beside the feast as though beside themselves. Then, grabbing a greedy hold, they wrench free a morsel and swim about, wolfing it down with gusto. After the picnic, before cleaning up, a few may do solo spins of satisfaction, if indeed that is what impels them.

Presently there is a common impulse to relax and rest, to stop spinning and to line up in rows like boats at a pier or with a few all facing each other as though moored to the same buoy, very chummily. They cease swimming as though stopped by some solid barrier. Besides braking with the depressible abdomen tip, they can backstroke with their four broad paddles that are thrust through the resistant surface film of the water.

In books on pond life you will see frequent references to this so-called surface film. There really isn't any film on the water. The surface has no skin. Water is all the same "to the last drop," from top to bottom. However, no matter how you stir it, whatever water happens to be at the top acts like a film because water is elastic; it tends to stretch, and its surface will bend before it breaks. Small lightweight insects dent but do not puncture it. Even a stone as wide as your hand will bounce off the water several times if you throw it properly. Whirligigs live supported by this "film," with their swimming legs thrust through it. And even as its tension gives good purchase to their paddles, it offers the necessary resistance when they wish to stop — and they stop very short.

The whirligigs leave one pond to fly to another. And they will leave your aquarium by air too, first climbing onto the raft or any perch above the water. So you will need a screen cover for it. Water beetles also leave the pond to hibernate ashore in mud or under decaying vegetation at the water's edge. But they rest lightly, and even in winter you may see a dytiscid or a hydrophilid swimming under the thin ice, protected by it from the cold air, the beetle's dark color absorbing warmth from the sun as through a pane of glass. If a thaw melts all the ice away, the restless gyrinids will waken and emerge for a midwinter frolic. Like the people who skated there but a week before, they go round and round, cutting fancy capers on the water, with every now and again one of them doing a pretty solo spin. In the late afternoon, as the sun's rays leave the pond with the possibility of ice forming even before dark, the whirligig socialites hastily depart to shelter in shore mud and rubbish.

Even when winter comes, you can go right on studying water beetles in an aquarium. If you have not set one up so far, it may still be possible before old Boreas begins to blow. Dytiscids will survive in an aquarium on a diet of raw beef for up to three years, depending on their age when captured.

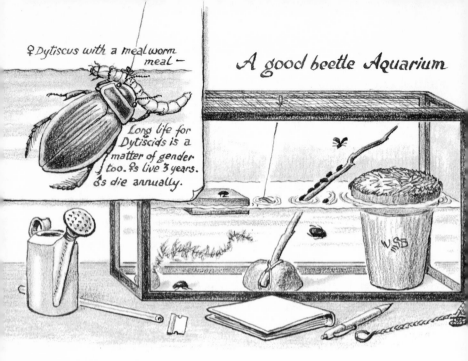

♀ Dytiscus with a mealworm meal —

Long life for Dytiscids is a matter of gender too. ♀s live 3 years. ♂s die annually.

They might eat other kinds of raw meat as eagerly, and other insects, if you can supply them.

Meal worms may be bought at pet stores. Suspend a live one by a thread at water level as an experiment. Or fry a beaten egg flat and firm with very little butter and no seasoning. When it cools, cut a little strip to hang like the meal worm. See if dytiscids take an interest. Gyrinids will and possibly hydrophilids. These last two kinds of water beetles will share an aquarium peaceably, but dytiscids must live alone as they are cannibals.

The straight-sided oblong aquariums are best. The water in these will always contain more life-improving dissolved air than that in any globe. And neither globes nor cylindrical glass tanks can be recommended for observing the behavior of the inhabitants, since such vessels distort the view so badly that frequently you cannot truly see what you are trying to record. With water in them, cylinders and globes become big lenses that bend light rays and make unrecognizable the things we see through their curving sides.

Bring home what water you can from the ponds where your beetles were caught, in glass or earthenware jugs, not in metal pails. Galvanized iron, brass, and copper containers will dissolve injurious chemicals into the water. If bringing pond water is impossible, use water from the tap. But run it well before taking any; it has been standing in galvanized or copper pipes. If your town water is chlorinated, boiling will get rid of the chlorine. After it cools, aerate it by pouring it back and forth from one container to another; wait until it is down to room temperature and then fill the aquarium about half full.

New wood will give out unhealthful acids in the water, so make your raft (for the hydrophilids to rest under and the gyrinids to rest on top of) from some old weather-beaten board. Try to set up the aquarium in a room where no coal or other gas fumes or oil heater fumes occur. Place it near a window where it will never receive more than an hour's direct sunlight daily. If it gets more, the water will become too warm for the good of the animals, while the sun speeds up the growth of plants, especially algae, which can become a nuisance.

As we have seen, water beetles like to fly from one pond to another, especially at night, and they will take off from the little aquarium raft or from an old dead twig you have peeled and anchored to a stone — with most of it sticking out of water for whirligigs to climb on. So cut a cover from some old window screen. Make it a half inch wider and longer than the top of your aquarium and bend down the edges to fit neatly over it.

So much for watching water beetles in the winter. But if, in summer, instead of grownup beetles, you happen to have captured a *Dytiscus* vampire dragon and a nearly as murderous hydrophilid larva, which you hope will become adults, it will be necessary to provide separate aquariums — and a going-ashore place where each can pupate after the first month of its life.

In the wild free state they would do this in the mud and rubbish of the pondside. As a substitute, you can prepare a flowerpot island for each of them. Put into each pot a layer of pebbles and fill it up with sand. Then get for each a carpet of moss — five inches across — from the shady bank of a woodland stream. Or cut from the lawn two circular pieces of turf the same size. Place these firmly over the sand and lower the island pots into the aquariums.

Keep the water level at about a half inch below the top rim of the pots, and one fine day both beetle grubs will crawl ashore and hole up under the moss or turf. In about two weeks you should find a sleek big beetle in each aquarium, perfect adults to watch and study and finally to prepare for your collection. Suppose you decide not to kill them but to extend the study period through the fall and winter. When pupation is over, you can remove the islands. Take them out, the better to watch the beetles without obstruction. Whirligigs sharing the *Hydrophilus* aquarium will not wish to cuddle under the island moss either while the indoor winter weather continues always warm. The raft will serve their need for sometimes getting out of water.

Do not cover the aquarium floor with sand or gravel or pebbles. Sand may be fine for fishes, but it is not needed for beetles, and gravel or pebbles are always bad because food particles, getting down among the little stones and out of the reach of feeding creatures, soon decay and foul the water. You can scrape some of the algae from the aquarium's sides with a single-edge razor blade if your hydrophilids and pond snails don't eat it fast enough.

For best results in watching water beetles, put in only a few plants or other objects, since they obscure the view. One water weed to clamber on and a little patch of duckweed will do. Don't crowd the stage with scenery. "The play's the thing"; every move your coleopterous characters make is what matters. The raft and the twig anchored to a stone are the only props gyrinids and hydrophilids need for occasionally drying off.

When suspending a bit of food at water level, tie one end of a thread around it and the other end in the mesh of the screen cover. Food not eaten the first day should be removed the second. On the third day feed the beetles again, and so on. To remove untouched crumbs, dead pond snails, or any other undesirable small object from the water, use a glass "dip tube" about ten inches long. Perhaps you can get a foot-long tube from the high-school chemistry teacher. Pet shops and biological supply houses have them for sale.

To lift a small object from the floor of the aquarium, place your thumb over the upper end of the tube to make it airtight and dip it down through the water till the lower end is close to and just above the object. No water has entered the tube, but when you lift your thumb, water rushes in at the bottom, drawing the object in with it. Cover the tube with your thumb again, airtight, and lift the tube. The water and object will come up right in the tube and will not run out until your thumb is raised again.

Water evaporates in a heated room, and more must be added from time to time. Be sure it is very nearly the same temperature as that in the aquarium. A sudden severe change can be fatal to the occupants. Use a small sprinkling can so that the water will carry fresh air in with it and yet stir up no currents to roil the water in the aquarium.

Keep a notebook handy and, like a good reporter, write down exactly what happens when your pet creatures do something that surprises or especially interests you. Be on the alert to see if it happens again under the same or different conditions. Keep the record. It may be more valuable than you think possible. What you see may not have been noticed by anyone before and may be the one piece needed to fill out some puzzle in man's knowledge of insects.

To Get the Most

To get the most good (in pleasure and profit) from reading natural history books, one also must observe Nature firsthand for one's self. To recognize something you see, having previously read about it, is gratifying. You are a witness. More than merely reading of an event, you are present when it happens. To observe something new, recorded in no book, is even more satisfying and exciting and increases your own personal information, at the same time adding to mankind's total knowledge regarding the manifold ways of life on this planet. Almost anyone taking an intelligent interest in insects may contribute something, however slight, to the science of entomology; so little is known as yet about so many com-

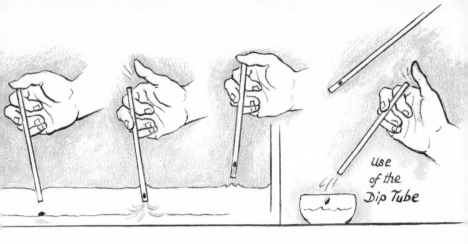

Use of the Dip Tube

mon species, so much is still to be discovered.

Therefore, observe insects to enhance your reading and read to aid your observations. This can involve you ever more deeply in nature lore, bringing into your own way of life the excellent habit of going afield often to watch creatures and possibly to capture a few of the "wee beasties" for a home insect zoo or an insect aquarium, wherein you can study matters more closely. Meanwhile, you may be gathering other specimens to preserve in an ever-growing home museum. If you want to tackle these projects, you should always have handy a small box or stoppered bottle for taking prizes come upon by happenstance in unlikely places; and you should take a pocket notebook wherever you go for on-the-spot recording of pertinent things observed. At home you will need a big loose-leaf notebook for pasting in all the small pages of your field notes and drawings and for entering your later ideas and even your fancies about the facts.

However inept your drawing may be, details of any insect studied and drawn will be registered more firmly in your mind than from long and careful looking with no attempt being made to depict it. Anyone who can form letters in writing can, with a little trying, copy the shapes, proportions, and special features of small objects such as insects. When you write and draw on paper what you have seen, you also engrave the same marks on your mind. Also, you are preparing a record that can always be consulted, a record helpful not only to yourself but possibly to other amateur entomologists and even to professionals in your correspondence, dealings, and discussions with them.

You will be dealing with other interested people, some in distant lands, as you and they seek to trade specimens of species not found locally, to fill out sets or series in a collection. You might form a beetling club in your own community, a "Club Coleoptera." Stamp collecting is a fine hobby, but few stamp collectors ever see firsthand all the countries from which their precious items come. Insect collectors can seek their prizes at the source, obtaining them at no cost on pleasant outings almost anywhere. They can raise some species from larvae or pupae, producing perfect undamaged specimens for themselves or for trade, gaining much more incidental information right at home from their own insect menageries.

Insect collecting is an inexpensive hobby within the means of almost anyone. Your State Museum library can furnish names and addresses of periodicals, put forth by various entomological societies, to which you can send for sample copies. Perhaps you may consult a naturalist's directory there, wherein are listed the names and addresses of many entomologists here and abroad, with the kinds of insects in which they specialize. Your public library will lend you books on insects. If it does not have books you especially wish to consult, see if the librarian can obtain them through an interlibrary system. Of course, where possible, buying books is better than borrowing. Then they remain with you to be used as tools of your trade.

Some authors advise beginners to collect every sort of insect that is available at first and begin to specialize later. But insects are so numerous and of so many widely differing types in their structure and habits that we are likely to learn only a little about any of them, to become confused, to miss the important facts, to lose our way in a fog of puzzles. It is

probably better to begin by confining our attention to a single group or order of insects, such as the Coleoptera, which illustrates all the basic insect characteristics while displaying a wide diversity of insect design and behavior. Then, having learned from the beetles the fundamental facts of insect life, we may branch out as we please, the better prepared to deal with other orders.

Most of the equipment needed for collecting and preserving insects can be made with very few materials. If you are not too good a "jackknife carpenter," ask the high-school biology teacher for the name and address of a biological supply house and send for its catalog. But if you are a handy do-it-yourselfer, perhaps you can follow directions for making your own apparatus, given in that booklet from the Superintendent of Documents (see p. 86), as well as in a variety of books on insects from the library. In these books the how-to-do-it chapters vary in details, but all their suggestions boil down to ways of outwitting the small game and approved methods of mounting specimens, arranging them, and caring for a collection.

A brief digest of this information (with additions) may be helpful here:

1. *Methods of Killing Specimens*

You will need a killing bottle for putting captured insects to sleep quickly and permanently without damaging their appearance. Materials and tools for rigging this apparatus are: the bottle, cotton, an unused blotter, some old window screening, chemicals, a pencil, a piece of chalk, and shears of some kind.

As to the chemicals proposed by various authors for killing specimens, each is objectionable in one respect or another. After all, each is a deadly poison, not meant to be attractive either as handled, inhaled, or swallowed by man or beast. When properly employed, they will kill an insect, and any one of them can kill a man if used improperly. All should be labeled POISON and kept where small children will not find them.

Many books recommend cyanide as the most effective anesthetic, but it is also the most dangerous and disagreeable.

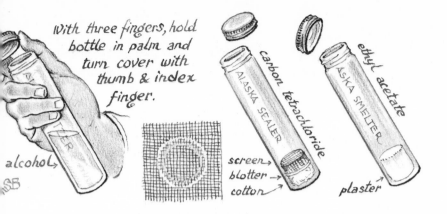

With three fingers, hold bottle in palm and turn cover with thumb & index finger.

alcohol

screen
blotter
cotton

carbon tetrachloride
ALASKA SEALER

ethyl acetate
ALASKA SMELTER

plaster

Others suggest carbon tetrachloride, which, though deadly, is so much safer to handle that it is sold in drugstores and supermarkets as a cleaning fluid called Carbona. Its bad feature is that it may change the colors of your specimens, especially the reds and yellows, if it comes in direct contact with them or if they remain in the fume-filled bottle long after they are dead.

One of the most easily obtained liquid killers is rubbing alcohol, into which a beetle simply may be dropped. But though some coleopterists emphasize its convenience and relative safety in handling, others object that it tends to swell a beetle's body, the bigger the beetle, the more distortion. This hazard may be greatly reduced if specimens are removed as soon as they are dead and not left in alcohol used as a preservative.

Ethyl acetate (acetic ether) is another readily procurable liquid, which has an advantage over all the other chemicals one may use. It "puts insects to sleep" in a relaxed condition, a very desirable quality. It will keep them relaxed if now and then you add a few drops in the closed jar where you keep them until they are mounted. It may be obtained at some drugstores or from a chemical or biological supply house, possibly with the kindly help of the high-school science teacher.

The killing bottle itself should be straight-sided (with no neck) and easy to open or close with the thumb and forefinger of the hand that holds it, while the other hand holds a captured prize ready to pop it in. Some entomologists prefer a bottle with a cork stopper, as the most easily opened in this manner. But the screw-on cover of an Alka-Seltzer bottle opens very easily with thumb and finger and does not leak when closed.

Killing bottles most suitable for work with beetles may contain carbon tetrachloride, ethyl acetate, or rubbing alcohol. For "carbon tet" (Carbona), put a wad of cotton into the bottom of an Alka-Seltzer bottle. Place an Alka-Seltzer tablet on a blotter, draw around it, and cut out — a hair's breadth outside the line — a blotting paper disk. Force this tight-fitting disk into the bottle with your thumb and push it down flat onto the cotton with the eraser end of a pencil.

Lay a Seltzer tablet on a piece of window screening about three inches square. Sharpen your chalk to a blunt point and draw a circle around the tablet on the screening. Remove the tablet and draw freehand another circle around the first one — about half an inch larger all around. Using tinsnips or a cheap pair of ordinary scissors, cut around the outer circle. Every quarter inch or so around the rim of this screen disk make cuts toward its center but stop each cut at the inner circle. Bend down all the tabs thus made and press the screen disk, tabs down, into the bottle. Push it down till the tabs touch the blotter disk.

The screen will prevent specimens from being discolored by direct contact with Carbona. Pour in just enough of this to saturate the cotton and blotter disk and close the bottle tightly. Keep it so at all times (except when dropping in or taking out specimens) in order to sustain the strength of the liquid, which evaporates rapidly when exposed to air.

For ethyl acetate, get a little plaster of Paris at a drugstore and mix it with enough water so that you can pour it into the bottom of an Alka-Seltzer bottle to the depth of an inch. Let the plaster set, then dry it thoroughly in the open bottle in an oven, heating it gradually. Let it cool and pour in enough ethyl acetate to soak the plaster through. Pour off any liquid the plaster does not absorb and close the bottle tightly. It will keep its potency for months if you keep it closed, and then you need only resaturate the plaster to recharge it.

But a coleopterist — a specialist in beetles — can do without cyanide, carbon tetrachloride, or ethyl acetate. If you intend to capture only beetles, half fill your bottle with rubbing alcohol and drop your specimens directly into it. No change will occur in the coloring of most species, especially the darker ones like June and ground beetles. But opalescent gems like tiger and Japanese beetles should be removed from the alcohol after an hour or two, allowed to dry off, and put away in a closed jar on dry blotters, under which are plenty of moth flakes, till such time as they can be mounted. The alcohol will not bloat your beetles in so short a time.

2. *Methods of Capture*

Many kinds of beetles may be caught in your hand — or in your handkerchief if, in fright, a specimen shows fight or

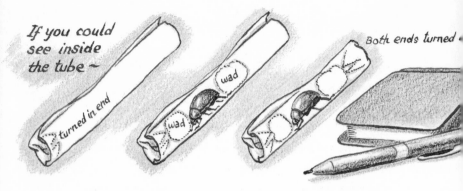

If you could see inside the tube ~

turned in end

wad

wad

Both ends turned ◂

emits an offensive odor. If an especially fine specimen appears unexpectedly and you make its capture in this way and don't have a tight little box or stoppered vial with you, put it, carefully wrapped in your handkerchief, into a shirt pocket. Tear a sheet from your pocket notebook and on it write the kind of beetle you think it is, the town near which you found it, the state, and the date. Give the specimen a number, which can be placed beside all future notes about it in your big loose leaf at home (weather at the hour of capture, where the beetle was and what it was doing, how it behaved before, during, and after being caught, and any thoughts — serious or facetious — you may have about it).

It is important to keep these data and the specimen always together so as to avoid errors and confused "remembering" later on. Roll this paper into a tube (on a pencil for a small beetle, on your finger for a bigger) and tuck one end in to close it and prevent unrolling. Make two dry paper wads and push one down the tube. Introduce the beetle next, followed by the other wad. Tuck in the open end behind it, and there is your specimen all wrapped up in its own data.

Put the little packet into a pocket — one on which you will not lean or sit. The insect will neither suffocate nor escape, and you can deal with it whenever you get home. Of course, if you do have your killing bottle handy when the beetle turns up unexpectedly, you are much better off. If you are purposely out seeking prizes, beetles on foliage — Japanese beetles, for example — can be caught directly in an alcohol bottle. Simply hold the open bottle just below a beetle and clap the cover over it. But much more can be accomplished with especially devised equipment. A net will bring in many kinds of beetles you otherwise would miss and make it possible to catch the more elusive beetles.

There are directions for making one's own nets in various insect books and pamphlets. Several types of net are recommended — for chasing insects on the wing, for sweeping field grass and shrubbery, and for similar work on and under water. Different fabrics are mentioned for the bags of several nets. But in every case the supporting hoop must be strong and strongly attached to the handle. Many prescribe a heavy steel wire for the hoop, but, except in the Government's booklet — "Collection and Preservation of Insects" — there is always a weakness in the way the wire hoop is attached to the wooden handle. The Government's booklet shows a strong attachment, but it calls for a ferrule — a metal sleeve — an article not easily made by amateurs unless they are equipped to cut a thick brass pipe. It also suggests that the hoop be tempered — a service not easily available since blacksmiths went out of style.

Brass pipe, heavy wire, tempering, none are necessary. Excellent nets can be made with the following materials:

the upper hoop from a nail keg
a pole one inch thick by three and a half feet long
an old window screen of copper or aluminum

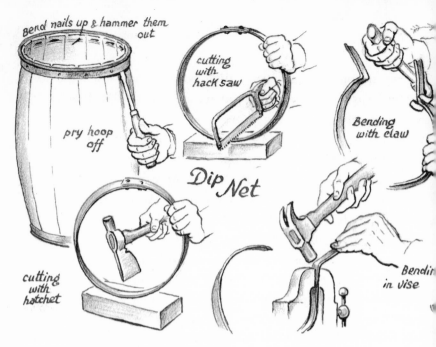

bend nails up & hammer them out

pry hoop off

cutting with hack saw

Bending with claw

Dip Net

cutting with hatchet

Bending in vise

a chunk of 2 x 4 lumber about six inches long

half a dozen 1½ inch galvanized shingle nails (the kind used for cedar roofing)

a roll of black adhesive tape

a spool of one ounce soft brass wire

a tenpenny nail

a half inch copper tack

Essential tools are: a claw hammer, hatchet, strong pliers, and an old screw driver.

Ask a lumber dealer, carpenter, or hardware merchant to save you an empty shingle nail keg. The metal hoop on either end of the keg is light but very strong. It is a tough steel ribbon with one edge rolled to form a stout tubular rim on the hoop. Let us call the flat remainder of the ribbon the apron. This ribbon with its rolled edge and flat apron is already bent in a perfect circle. With your claw hammer remove the several nails that hold the keg's upper hoop — the hoop at the open end — and with your screw driver pry the hoop up and off.

Hold the hoop down on your chunk of 2 x 4, or other wooden block, and cut through the hoop at a point opposite its rivets. The apron could be cut with the tinsnips, but the tubular rim is just too tough; so use a hacksaw or the edge of a file or give it a few hard chops with a hatchet. Now bend out at right angles the first five inches of the cut ends. Do this with your hammer claw. Place the claw over the hoop's rim five inches from a cut end. Now, with one hand holding the hoop firmly against your chest, grasp the hammer handle near its tip in the other hand and pull down. The claw will bite the tough rolled rim and your long grip on the hammer handle will give good leverage. The hoop will resist, but it will give. Bend the other cut end in the opposite direction.

If you cannot bend the ends this way but have a work bench with a vise, put the hoop in the vise with five inches of one end facing up. Pull back and down on the cut end while hammering it just above the vise at the point where it is to bend at a right angle. Bend the other end in the other direction.

There are holes in the apron at about six-inch intervals, put there for the cooper's convenience in nailing the hoop to the wooden staves of the keg. None of the holes may be in quite the right place for our purpose of nailing the bent-out apron ends to the handle of the net. So lay one apron end on your wooden block and, about one and a quarter inches from the bend, punch a hole with a sharp tenpenny nail and your hammer. Do not drive in the shank of the nail. Merely make

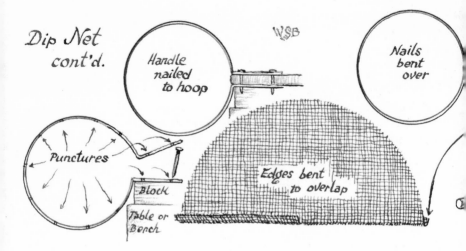

WSB

Handle
nailed
to hoop

Nails
bent
over

Punctures

Block

Table or
Bench

Edges bent
to overlap

a puncture through which a smaller nail can be driven. Make another puncture about three quarters of an inch from the bent apron's outer end. While you are at it, punch extra holes in the apron all around the hoop so that, with the holes already made by the keg coopers, you will have a hole at least every three inches.

The three and one-half foot handle should be an inch thick stick of reasonably soft wood recently cut and peeled, not an old broom or hoe handle, hard and brittle. Place it between the bent apron ends and, holding all down on the wood block, drive one and one-half inch galvanized nails (used for cedar shingling) through the two punctures in the upper apron, through the handle, and right on through the other apron underneath. The nails will penetrate if you hit hard and true. The aprons and handle are now nailed not only together but also to the wood block. With your screw driver pry them from the block; then turn the net handle around and, again holding against the wood block, hammer the protruding nail ends snugly over. You will have a ten and one-half inch hoop with a three and one-half foot handle.

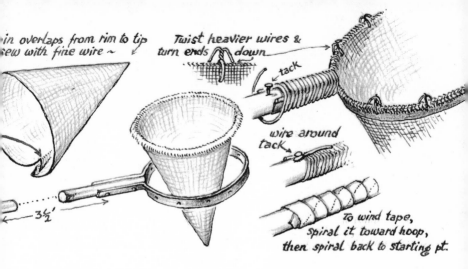

in overlaps from rim to tip
sew with fine wire ~

Twist heavier wires &
turn ends down

tack

wire around
tack

3½'

To wind tape,
spiral it toward hoop,
then spiral back to starting pt.

Suppose this is to be a water or dip net. From an old copper or aluminum screen cut a half circular piece with a twelve-inch radius as pictured. Unravel a fine wire from the screen's straight edge. At the center of the straight edge make a quarter-inch cut. With your fingers bend a quarter inch of the screen's edge on one side, away from you, and a quarter inch on the other side toward you. Tap the two bent edges flat with your hammer. When the two edges are brought together to form a cone, one bent-over edge can be fitted into the other and the two sewn flat against the cone with the fine wire unraveled from the straight edge.

Set the cone inside the hoop leaving three-quarters of an inch margin to bend over the hoop all around, overlapping the holes in the apron. Through these holes fasten cone to hoop with heavier "thread" from your spool of one-ounce soft brass wire. Cut the ends of your twisted wires with the wire cutter in the jaws of your pliers, or with the shears, and bend them against the hoop so that they won't catch on water weeds.

Take two turns of brass wire around the handle where the

screening overlaps it and twist the wire tight. Put a half-inch copper tack half of its length into the handle between the very ends of the bent aprons. Wind the wire you have just twisted over the screening on the handle, round and round, tightly spiraling down the handle to the apron ends. Coil it about the tack and drive the tack home. Cut your tacked wire from the spool and bend the stump back against the spiral. Starting on the handle an inch beyond the apron ends, wind firmly over all (handle, aprons, spiral wire) your black adhesive tape till you reach the hoop. Keep winding but return down the handle, each turn overlapping the last, till you are back where you started.

The dip net is ready for hard use. It is stout enough to serve momentarily as a pole or paddle in working a boat through weedy waters or as a cane and a balancer when stumbling through bogland to reach a body of water. It will not be overstrained if you scoop up heavy bottom mud. When you do this, bring the laden net just to the surface and sweep it from side to side. Much mud will wash away, but its population will remain. You can transfer the catch to a pan of

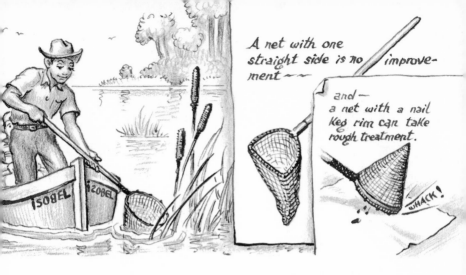

A net with one straight side is no improvement ~~

and — a net with a nail keg rim can take rough treatment.

WHACK!

ISOBEL ISOBEL

water to cull out the creatures you don't want, though it may be easier simply to spread part of an old sheet in the boat or ashore and empty a few "critters" onto it at a time.

Dislodge any little fellows still clinging in the net with a good thwack of its rim against the sheet on the boat bottom or the ground. It won't hurt this net at all. Have two jars of water ready. Put *Dytiscus* dragons in one, separate from the rest, because even in the confusion of sudden captivity, their voracious appetites will prompt them to attack and ruin your other prizes.

Instructions in some books advocate a hoop flattened on the outer side, forming a half moon instead of a circular opening, for a dip net. This idea is based on the notion that one will be dredging a smooth bottom relatively clear of weeds, rocks, roots, and other obstructions. But such clear areas are equally clear of creatures. You will not be working there. A circular net will bring better results in all situations. Sweep it among the water weeds near shore from the bottom to the surface of the pond. If it comes up empty, hold it above the water ready to swoop and make no move. Presently, tak-

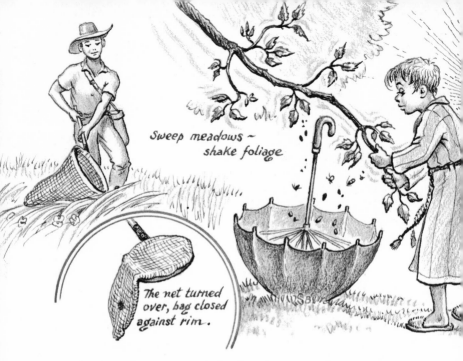

Sweep meadows ~
shake foliage

The net turned over, bag closed against rim.

ing you for a part of the inanimate setting, water creatures (stirred up by the net but soon forgetting it) will rise for air. Wait till a prize beetle or larva pushes one end through the "film," but wait no more; it will breathe but an instant, so dip swiftly.

To make a foliage sweeper or a hot-pursuit net, all you need to do differently, after fastening hoop to handle, is to attach the longer fabric bags described in the Government booklet and various insect books — heavy muslin or light canvas for sweeping; marquisette or bobbinet for tearing after tiger beetles by day or making swoops at the many kinds that flit about street lights on summer nights.

In sweeping for beetles, walk slowly in a meadow, moving the net in long arcs just low enough to stroke the grasses first on your left, then on your right. Keep the net moving and, every six or seven strokes, turn it with your wrist so that the

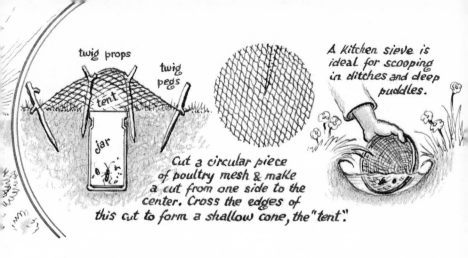

twig props

twig pegs

tent

jar

A kitchen sieve is ideal for scooping in ditches and deep puddles.

Cut a circular piece of poultry mesh & make a cut from one side to the center. Cross the edges of this cut to form a shallow cone, the "tent."

cloth will lie across and cover the rim, preventing escape while you inspect and reach in to remove your catch. Sweep dense shrubbery similarly. Turn the net as just described the instant you catch a precious beetle on the wing or you may lose it, perhaps after a long and hot pursuit. If making your own net seems too difficult, you can buy an all-purpose net with a nylon mesh bag from a biological supply house.

Spread your old piece of sheeting on the ground under a bush or the low branch of a tree and beat the bush with a short stick or shake the branch vigorously. You may be astonished at the number and variety of insects that shower down. Or hold a light-colored umbrella open and upside down below the branches you are about to jar and jiggle. A dark background is not good for sorting the specimens you will be getting. A good time for this type of hunting is just after daybreak while the insects are still cool and sleepy.

Beetles can be trapped in wide-necked glass jars buried overnight up to their rims in the earth. A teaspoonful or two of molasses in the bottom will attract the insects and hold them till you make your morning rounds; you will have to soak and rinse and rinse your specimens in warm water to unstick the molasses, but it may be well worth the trouble.

Beetles will come, but you will have to adopt measures for keeping other animals away. If no wild animals prowl your neighborhood after dark (you might be surprised at the number of skunks, weasels, opossums, foxes, and raccoons that still do), there are always dogs and cats and rats that will carry off carrion meant only for various interesting beetles. Many animals have a sweet tooth too and will trouble your molasses bottle-traps or claw the beetles already in them.

So spread tents of one-inch mesh poultry netting over your baits, pegging them as pictured. This will let beetles pass in easily but will baffle bigger beasts. A tent must extend far enough on all sides so that reaching creatures cannot hook the bait with their claws. If rain threatens, lean a short board on the wire over the trap on the side from which wet weather usually comes, and weight it with a brick or rock.

For luring carrion and burying beetles, pick up on a stick — and carry in a covered shoe box — the dead body of any small animal you may find. If you are a fisherman, the smallest fish in your creel or the head of the largest will make good beetle bait. Perhaps you can trap some mice. Or maybe your cat will offer you a few. A well-fed feline is likely to try sharing its catch with human friends. Experiment with a piece of Limburger or other strong cheese. Of course, flies will come by day, and they will be followed by those "child (or larva) lovers," the maggot-eating rove beetles and others. But see if burying beetles will deem it worthy of their attention.

You can collect a variety of light-happy beetles among the moths at your window screens on summer evenings. In pastures by day, our relatives of Cleopatra's Coleoptera trundle their treasures, while rove beetles run about seeking grubs to devour. In all manner of outdoor places, on foliage and flowers, on and under the bark of trees — standing or fallen — under rocks and rubbish, in the earth and in the water of roadside ditches, almost anywhere, there may be a beetle or its larvae. Water beetles in ditches and big puddles can be scooped up with a kitchen sieve, where a dip net might be too large.

The height of the beetle-collecting season is in the hottest months of summer, but you can begin active beetling in the spring. April Fool's Day may bring your first specimens — ladybird beetles easily sighted on the budding shrubbery. Even before that a few ladybirds may be awake trying to get outdoors through your windowpanes. By May Day you can dig up June beetles if you spade the garden then. On hillsides facing south, warmed by the sun, you can find bombardiers and a few other ground beetles by overturning rocks, especially the flatter rocks, old boards and other such favorite "roofs."

With the start of June, various beetles other than ladybirds may attempt to pass through your window glass at night. As they try to reach your reading light, you will hear sharp whacks on the glass, very different from the thuds of heavy soft-bodied moths. Hurry out with a ready handkerchief or a drinking glass and any piece of stiff paper you can snatch. There on the sill you may see such a prize as the shovel-faced, scarab-like dung beetle *Copris tullius* Oliv., formerly called *Copris anaglypticus* Say. Place the glass over the beetle and slip the paper between it and the window sill or whatever the beetle happens to be on. Hold paper and

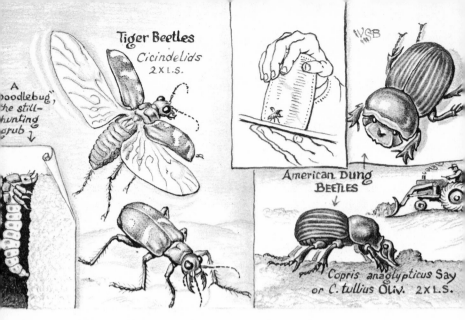

Tiger Beetles
Cicindelids
2 X L.S.

A "doodlebug", the still-hunting grub ↓

WGB

American Dung BEETLES
↓

Copris anaglypticus Say
or *C. tullius* Oliv. 2X L.S.

glass together while you carry off the prize to your killing jar. Or better, put it into a loosely covered Mason jar half full of damp soil or sand and observe its digging technique. Once it has dug in, it will do little else while you are watching. It only does this much to get out of sight. But it is wonderful to watch the manner in which it lowers its clypeus, the spade-shaped shield on its face, and thrusts it down into the soil, forward and up like a veritable power shovel, the big spikes on its rear legs giving it as good a purchase for its size as the heavy ridges on the tires of a tractor. What a powerful set of muscles it must have to root up so much soil in so short a time! In a moment it is entirely concealed.

Make it a practice as regular as walking the dog to go out each night before heading for bed and inspect every window of your home behind which a light is still burning.

Of course, you can set a light trap outdoors to burn all night long. It will catch a mess of insects, possibly a third of them likely to be beetles. Various types of light traps may be bought from biological supply houses. These traps can be homemade too, but they are rather too complicated contraptions for most do-it-yourself-ers. The basic idea is to have a pane of glass in front of a light, so slanted that it deflects all insects colliding with it downward and into a killing liquid below the light. There is a trap on the market now that uses a light with suction (no poison, no gum-stickum). It catches quarts of insects between sundown and morning.

Don't overlook the opportunities for netting many species of beetles flying about street lamps even on rainy nights and crawling on the ground beneath.

By day go into pastures if you are fortunate enough to live near them. Keep a sharp eye out for tumblebugs and see what other species you can spy about "cow platters." If you wish to open an old fallen and rotted tree or its stump, strike your hatchet in with the grain, not across it, and pry to one side. A good sheath knife will do as well or better than the hatchet, but such work is weakening to the joints of even the stoutest jackknife. Move along the grain, taking out the punk, chunk by chunk, and being ready to snatch any beetle that may show.

If, as you walk along a sandy path, pencil-wide holes suddenly appear in the ground, you have located tiger beetle larvae's dwellings. They stopper these holes with their flat earth-colored heads, their jaws open and ready to snap shut on any passing insect. But they back down out of sight at your approach. You can catch them one at a time with a garden trowel. Kneeling with an empty quart Mason jar close by and your trowel at the ready, wait till a foolish larva comes up and resets its head at the top of its hole; then make a lightning jab close to it, bringing up a trowelful of soil containing the creature, and dump it into the jar.

At home fill a second quart jar with damp sand to a depth of four inches. Make a pencil hole about two inches deep in the middle of the sand. Make a dozen nail holes in a screw-on metal lid for the jar. Your tiger-beetle terrarium is ready. Never leave it in direct sunlight or it will heat up and become unhealthful — and the grub for which you made it will die. When slid from the first jar into the second, the grub will quickly dodge into the pencil hole and bore on down to the jar's bottom. It can't get out of the open jar while still an *enfant terrible,* but keep the jar covered to prevent its prey from escaping when you feed it, and also later to keep the grown-up beetle in the jar when it comes out of its pupal sleep.

After a day in the jar, undisturbed, the terrible trapper will be up stoppering the pencil hole with its head, jaws opened wide and waiting for a victim. Drop into the jar a tent caterpillar or a buffalo bug or perhaps a small angleworm. Try flies and other insects, one kind at a time, including the big gray "stink bugs" that are common on squash plants. See if the little living trap snaps shut on all kinds automatically, showing no preferences, or if it snatches but then rejects some kinds. Never offer as food insects that have been exposed to insect poisons such as DDT. Feed the miniature wild beast some sort of prey once every few days. If it pupates successfully, you will have a perfect tiger beetle in a few weeks, perhaps more easily obtained this way than by chasing such brisk fliers as the adults are with a net. Put the tiger beetle that pupates from your grub to sleep so that you can get it out of the jar without the risk of losing it. To do so, drop a dab of cotton soaked with Carbona into the jar, taking care not to get any on the beetle, and cover it tightly with an unpunctured screw-on top. Be as deft when switching covers as a magician shifting nutshells in the old pea game.

When winter comes, you can continue beetling in various ways. Water beetles will continue active in the warmth of your home. Of course, if you live in or travel to a part of the country where the climate remains mostly mild, you can carry on just as you would during a summer farther north. Yet even in an area where the winter months are pretty cold, though all outdoor species are snug in their hideaways or frozen dead, you still can buy meal worms, the children of flour beetles — *Tenebrio molitor* Linn. — at pet shops. They are not pets but pests, though useful enough as food for pet birds, toads, and lizards. But the pet-shop man will show you how to keep them in a jar almost full of torn bits of newspaper with corn meal or whole-wheat flour sprinkled all between.

The jar should be placed in some dim-lit corner and covered with a screen or at least with a piece of cheesecloth tied over it, in case any worms pupate and then become beetles sooner than expected. They usually pupate in spring, but there are always likely to be individuals in a group that tend to deviate from the rules. In the warmth of winter in your home, not a few might be ready for the big change rather early, possibly in March.

The worms are yellowish or light brown, but the pupae are white and will be found lying loose among the paper scraps. About ten days after pupation begins, you should have some shiny black beetles almost three-quarters of an inch in length. These flour beetles are most active after dark. The so-called Black Beetles, which are sometimes a pest in houses, are not beetles at all but big cockroaches.

Keep a ventilating cover over the jar lest, some spring night, specimens escape while you are sleeping. This would be an annoying loss to you and could become the cause of really serious losses later, in granaries and stored cereal bins and bakeries, where your beetles, getting in, would lay their eggs. Sift into the jar a little more meal or flour for your captive nuisances from time to time if, on inspection, they seem to be running short. If you see signs of mildew in their remaining food, do not worry. They seem to favor and somehow benefit from a diet of moldy meal. If not removed from the jar, your new generation of adult flour beetles will lay eggs in it, and soon there will be a very numerous fresh supply of meal worms rattling among the paper scraps. They don't need water, being quite comfortable with their own metabolic moisture.

3. *Methods of Mounting and Preserving Beetles*
   You will need the following:
   corrugated cardboard
   a tube of transparent, quick-drying cement, such as Duco
   a tube of rubber cement for paper
   a bottle of waterproof India ink
   linen writing paper
   a small piece of Bristol board
   some No. 3 black Japan mounting pins (from a biological
      supply house)

masking tape

a single-edge razor blade or sharp jackknife

a ruler and pencil

a shoe box

moth flakes

rubbing alcohol

medicine vials

And for safe keeping, you must have snugly closing boxes of some sort. Either you can buy regular cabinet trays from a biological supply house or, for a start at least, you can use cigar boxes and keep them in a bureau drawer, the drawer well sprinkled with moth flakes. The cabinet trays come with sliding glass covers. But glass is not essential, since you will always keep collection containers closed except when working at or showing your specimens.

The older insect books call for layers of cork in your boxes and trays of mounted specimens. Today cork is a scarce article, but an excellent replacement is available everywhere. Corrugated cardboard can be used very well instead. The aim is to have a neat and safe place to house your collection, each specimen labeled with its generic and specific names, the town and state where it was found, the month and the year.

You will need cigar boxes that hold fifty cigars, about two inches deep. The number 50 is always printed on them somewhere, often on the underside. The best boxes are made entirely of wood with a cover that closes over a ridge on the outside of the box; they have metal hinges and a hasp to keep them closed.

The cheaper boxes are partly wood and paper and very

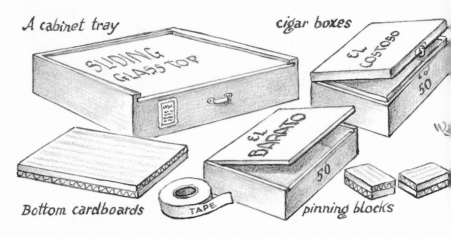

A cabinet tray   cigar boxes

SLIDING GLASS TOP

EL COSTOSO

EL BARATO

Bottom cardboards   TAPE   pinning blocks

tough cardboard, and the cover fits inside the box ends, resting on the upper edge of the box front. These may be made pest-proof with strips of masking tape, which is easily removed when boxes must be opened.

Cut a flat sheet of corrugated cardboard to fit neatly into the cigar-box bottom, with the corrugations running lengthwise, and another the same size with the corrugations crosswise. When cut in this way and stuck together with quick drying household cement, these pieces will not warp. Do not spread the cement like jam in a sandwich but put one dab on each corner and in the center of each piece. Put the glued sides face to face with the edges even and lay them on a table under heavy books, or any flat weight, till dry. Make several little two-layered pinning blocks — about 2 x 3 inches — in the same manner.

When the double-layered cardboard is dry, strew moth flakes liberally in the box and press the cardboard flatly in on top of them. Plenty of moth flakes should be used at all times; museum pests never give up looking for a place to begin. Keep the cigar box closed now, even though no mounted specimens are in it yet.

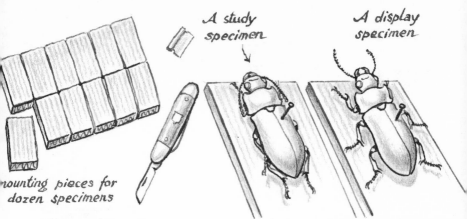

Cut one more sheet of corrugated board the size of the box bottom less an eighth of an inch in width and length. Divide this into twelve equal oblongs (about $1\frac{5}{16}$ inches x $2\frac{5}{8}$ inches) and cut them apart with a single-edge razor blade or a sharp jackknife. Do this with the cardboard lying on a bread board; do not try to cut the stiff material while holding it up in your hand. Each of these small pieces is the mount on which to pin a beetle and paste its label. You are now ready to pose your first beetle.

Whether your specimens met their end in alcohol or a Carbona killing bottle, if they have dried and stiffened, they must be relaxed before they can be mounted; otherwise, legs and antennae will break off when you try to set them in the best position. The best position for appendages of a "study" (not a "display") specimen is lying back along the body, which affords them some protection. For a display case they should be arranged in a more active pose, as seen when a living beetle moves along. The appendages are important in determining to what species a specimen belongs. The form and number of tiny sections, or segments, in the antennae and the number of parts forming the feet, or tarsi, are telling features.

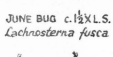

JUNE BUG c.1½X L.S.
Lachnosterna fusca

Dorsal or
upper side
showing scutellum
and point where pin
should enter.

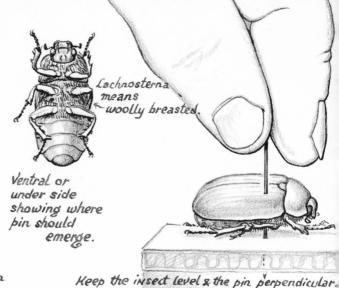

Lachnosterna
means
← *woolly breasted.*

Ventral or
under side
showing where
pin should
emerge.

Keep the insect level & the pin perpendicular.

Beetles can be relaxed in a bottle rigged like the Carbona killing bottle as described earlier but with the cotton and blotter disk saturated with water only. Add a few drops of Chlorox or Lysol to prevent mildew, slide your dead beetles down onto the screen disk, and close the bottle tightly. In a few days (one day for small beetles, two or three for bigger), they will be pliant and may be mounted with no trouble. Many books call for a teaspoonful of carbolic acid dissolved in a quart of water (a few drops of this added to the wet cotton in the bottle) to prevent mildew. But carbolic acid is a very dangerous poison and is not really needed. One must be careful with Chlorox and Lysol, but they are much safer to use and just as effective.

Let us say you are about to mount a June bug, a big beetle easy to handle and generally common in almost every area of the country. Hold it on a pinning block and push a No. 3 black Japan pin straight down through the right wing cover (the elytrum) and the body (so that it comes out on the right

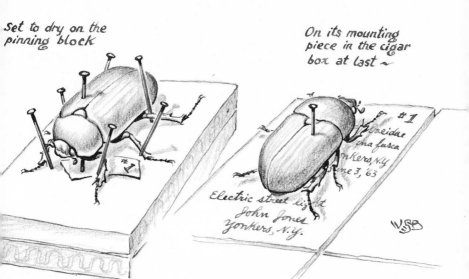

Set to dry on the pinning block

On its mounting piece in the cigar box at last ⁓

#1

Scaraeidae
*na fusca
nkers, N.Y
ne 3, 63

#1

Electric street light
John Jones
Yonkers, N.Y.

WSB

of center between the second and third leg) into the block. Press on the pin until its head is within a half inch of the beetle.

Many kinds of insects should be pinned through the thorax, but beetle species are identified partly by details of the scutellum, that somewhat triangular tidbit of chitin between the wing covers where they hinge onto the thorax; therefore, beetles are never pinned through the middle but through the right elytrum instead.

Now raise the mounting pin, with the beetle on it, just enough to allow for opening the folded legs, one leg at a time. With a second pin move the right hind leg out till it looks "natural" and push this pin into the cardboard between the leg and body to bar the leg from folding under again, as it tends to do even though "relaxed." Balance the pull of this mounted right hind leg by setting its opposite, the left hind leg, in a similar position. Now set the middle pair, then the forward pair of legs, and finally the feelers.

The feelers on a June beetle are short and are pressed close to the face in death. If, after being relaxed, they still resist, do not force them out till they break. If one of them does break off at the point of attachment to the face, stick it to the label with a drop of clear quick-drying cement. If longer, more conspicuous feelers break off, they can be reattached to the face in an alert position, using the same kind of cement. Legs can be replaced, but be sure to attach them "as Nature intended," which can be ascertained by a careful look at the remaining legs on the specimen.

Pinned on its block, the beetle should be set in a covered shoe box with a good handful of moth flakes to dry in the pose you have given it. Leave it there at least a week, for unless completely dry when finally placed in the cigar box, it will not hold its pose. Write "No. 1" on a slip of paper and stick it temporarily to the pin under the beetle. Keeping its correct number always with a specimen is even more necessary when preparing several at the same time.

In the meanwhile, write its label as far as your information goes. In this case you already know that a June beetle is of the scarab family. So write "Scarabaeidae," then the genus *"Lachnosterna"* and the species *"fusca"* (if that is what you have), then the town near which you found it, the state, and the date, plus "#1."

Identifying and classifying your beetles will be like laboratory detective work. There are keys or lists of clues to aid you. These are published by your state museum or state university. They describe every insect known to that region of the country. But using these keys can be tedious and troublesome to a beginner. You first find out everything a specimen is not, until (from the traits left that do fit your beetle) you can definitely say that it is a male of such and such a family, genus, and species.

As for your June bug, a very helpful book published by the U.S. Department of Agriculture in March of 1953 is "May Beetles of the United States and Canada" by Luginbill and Painter (Technical Bulletin No. 1060). It is no longer to be had from the Government Printing Office, but the Superintendent of Documents will send you a free list of libraries in your state where you can probably see a copy. Besides life histories, the book has maps showing in which states each species is found, with keys for classifying May beetle species of the three genera, *Melolontha, Lachnosterna,* and *Phyllophaga,* and with descriptions and photographs of many.

Identifying is something like the old guessing game that starts, "Is it animal or vegetable or mineral?" But this is a game that veteran entomologists frankly say does not become easy to play until you have had years of experience. So just do your best, make good mounts, and some day get permission to show them to a professional entomologist. He can help identify them and just possibly, in the process, you will find at least one new species or variety — most gratifying to both amateur and professional.

Make your label by cutting a piece of good linen writing paper to cover the little cardboard on which the beetle will be mounted. Write all the data you have, plus the specimen's number, in India ink on this white paper. Stick it to the cardboard mount with rubber cement. The latter does not shrink in drying and allows easy removal of the label if corrections are needed later. Set the labeled cardboard among the eleven other little pieces in the cigar box. When the beetle is dry, gently pull out all the pins that have held things in place (except the main mounting pin through the body). Pull the mounting pin from the block with the beetle on it and, placing the pin's point a little to the right of center of the labeled piece in the cigar box, push it down as perpendicularly as you can through the labeled piece and the double layer of corrugated board till it touches the wooden bottom of the box. The beetle will be far enough up the pin so that the label can be read below it. Try to set all your specimens at the same level in the box to have a good-looking collection. Close the box and keep it in a bureau drawer where it has been snowing moth flakes. Your beetle museum, though it consists so far of only one specimen, is started.

One cannot pin the smaller beetles. A ladybird must be mounted on a little piece of stiff white card cut the shape of an apple seed but twice the size. Push a No. 3 mounting pin through the wider end of this cutout and stop when within half an inch of the pin head. Put a drop of clear quick-drying cement on the cutout's pointed end, to the left of the pin, and set the ladybird, belly down, in it. Make a label to put on this beetle's little corrugated cardboard mounting piece and push down the pin with the specimen on the bit of card, just as you did the pin holding the June beetle.

Perhaps you will wish to preserve specimens of the larvae of the beetles you mount. These can be "pickled" in rubbing alcohol in little medicine vials and the data written in pencil on slips of paper, placed carefully in the vials so the writing faces out and can be read. But the soft-bodied larvae will col-

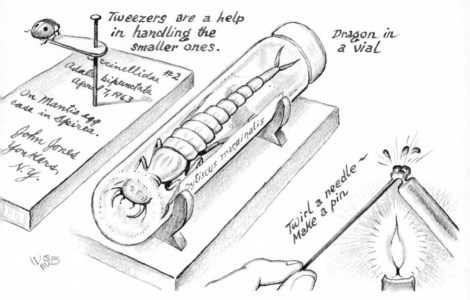

Tweezers are a help in handling the smaller ones.

Coccinellidae #2
Adalia bipunctata
April 7, 1963

On Mantis egg case in Spirea.

John Jones
Yonkers, N.Y.

Dragon in a vial

Dytiscus marginalis

Twirl a needle ~
Make a pin

WSB

lapse and shrivel if introduced directly into the alcohol. Put them first in a well-shaken bottle of half rubbing alcohol and half water. After about five hours they may be transferred to the undiluted alcohol. There is yet another hazard. Some white grubs tend to turn black in alcohol unless they are dipped for a minute or so in boiling water before being put into the first alcohol-and-water mixture. Carefully pickled, a water dragon (that blood-sucking grub of *Dytiscus*) will look as predatory in clear alcohol as in its native pond.

Here are a few more helpful hints. If you are out of standard mounting pins, make some by twirling the eye end of No. 7 sharp sewing needles in bubbling hot sealing wax. It will take several twirlings and coolings to get a good knob on a needle, but it will become a fine pin. You won't burn your fingers and thumb if you hold the needle near the point end while twirling.

When writing for the first time to an entomologist whose name you have found in *The Naturalist's Directory*, if you are unknown to him, enclose return postage, especially if he lives outside of the United States. An International Reply Coupon can be obtained at any U.S. Post Office and costs fifteen cents no matter in what foreign land the scientist lives. At his own post office the coupon pays for postage on his reply.

If your letters lead to exchanging specimens of beetles, they can be sent without damage if properly packed. They are handled as merchandise, so no correspondence should be enclosed, and the package should be done up strongly. Use stout boxes and wrapping paper. To send unmounted beetles, put a layer of cotton batting in the bottom of the box. Cover this with tissue paper and lay the beetles on the tissue, none touching another. Cover them with a second tissue and on top of this enough cotton batting to fill the box so that it requires a little pressure to close it.

For sending mounted specimens, as for example a dozen in a cigar box, first tie the box cover tight. You will need a well-made cardboard carton about two inches bigger all around than the cigar box. Pack the space between the inner and outer boxes with good springy excelsior, top, bottom, ends, and sides, wrap and tie well, and write the address and return address as you do on any parcel post package. A good plan is to add "Natural History Specimens — Fragile — Handle with Care."

If you should care to read further about beetles, the following books and pamphlets may be useful, especially to beginners:

1. *How to Know the Beetles* by H. E. Jaques, William C. Brown Co., Dubuque, Iowa

2. *A Manual of Common Beetles of Eastern North America* by Dillon and Dillon, Row, Peterson & Co., Evanston, Ill.
3. *Field Book of Insects* by Frank E. Lutz, G. P. Putnam's Sons, New York, N.Y.
4. *Handbook of Nature Study* by Anna Botsford Comstock, Comstock Publishing Co., Inc., Ithaca, N.Y.
5. *Insect Life* by John Henry Comstock, Comstock Publishing Co., Inc., Ithaca, N.Y.
6. *Hammond's Guide to Nature Hobbies* by Emil Leopold Jordan, C. S. Hammond & Co., New York, N. Y.
7. *The Naturalist's Directory,* P.C.L. Publications, Box 282, Phillipsburg, N.J.
8. *4-H Club Entomology Leader's Manual,* 1956, 16 p., il., 20¢, Government Printing Office Catalog No. A1. 76:106
9. *4-H Club Insect Manual,* 1954, 64 pp., il., 30¢, Government Printing Office Catalog No. A1. 76:65

This book has described only some of the interesting things that are known about a few kinds of beetles. It is impossible to consider every species in one volume. There are so many in the world that a simple catalog of them (giving merely the name, location, and books or papers wherein a species is discussed) fills thirty-one fat volumes. If each species had been described and illustrated in the catalog, it would have been several hundred volumes long.

But this is one of the reasons why collecting beetles is such a good hobby. They are so numerous that you need never return empty-handed from a field trip. One insect species in every three in the world is a beetle of some sort. And beetles make a fine display, not in the manner of moth and butterfly collections (the charm of the latter is somewhat like the attraction of fine feathers) but appealing to us, in some species, more as beautiful gems and in others as fascinating and incredible grotesqueries. There seems to be no limit to their variety or to the new facts one can learn about them. Consider a very few of the kinds of beetles and their ways we have not even touched upon.

There is not one word in this book about the numerous Leaf Beetles, and the clever Leaf-Roller Weevils, which make cigars to house their larvae, nor the Hister, Blister, and Oil Beetles. We have said nothing of the Crawling Water Beetles or of the tiny blind ones that live like waterproofed fleas in the fur of beavers.

Besides these, there are the ant-loving beetles called Pselaphidae, the sap-feeding Nitidulidae, and the checkered Cleridae and many others. We have not mentioned the Darkling Beetles of the West, which, when you lift their stone, stand almost on their heads while stalking stiffly about, stinking in offensive defense. We have not raised the question, "How does the Click Beetle click?" Equally competent entomologists will give you opposite answers. Why not see for yourself? Hold a click beetle up by its abdomen and watch the underside of its thorax. Notice the spine that fits into a groove there. Does the beetle bend backward and then suddenly forward, jabbing the spine into the groove to make the click? Or does it first bend forward to set the spine in the tight-fitting groove and then pull powerfully back till the spine comes loose, allowing the head and thorax suddenly to snap back? In your hand not much of a click is audible, but with the beetle lying on its back on a hard wood table, there is a sharp sound. Does this show that it clicks, not by hitting for-

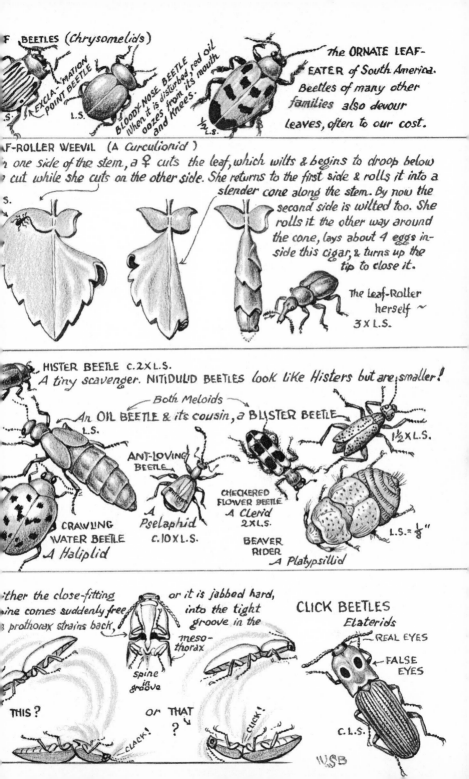

F BEETLES *(Chrysomelids)*

EXCLA-MATION POINT BEETLE

L.S.

.S.

BLOODY-NOSE BEETLE, red oil oozes from its mouth and knees, when it is disturbed

½ L.S.

The ORNATE LEAF-EATER of South America. Beetles of many other families also devour leaves, often to our cost.

F-ROLLER WEEVIL (A *Curculionid*)

n one side of the stem, a ♀ cuts the leaf, which wilts & begins to droop below cut while she cuts on the other side. She returns to the first side & rolls it into a slender cone along the stem. By now the second side is wilted too. She rolls it the other way around the cone, lays about 4 eggs inside this cigar, & turns up the tip to close it.

S.

The Leaf-Roller herself ~ 3 X L.S.

HISTER BEETLE C. 2 X L.S.
A tiny scavenger. NITIDULID BEETLES *look like Histers but are smaller!*

— Both Meloids →
An OIL BEETLE & its cousin, a BLISTER BEETLE

L.S.

1½ X L.S.

ANT-LOVING BEETLE

CHECKERED FLOWER BEETLE
A Clerid
2 X L.S.

A Pselaphid
c. 10 X L.S.

CRAWLING WATER BEETLE
A Haliplid

BEAVER RIDER
A Platypsyllid

L.S. = ⅛"

---

ther the close-fitting ine comes suddenly free, prothorax strains back,

or it is jabbed hard, into the tight groove in the meso-thorax

spine in groove

CLICK BEETLES
Elaterids

REAL EYES

FALSE EYES

THIS?

or THAT ?

CLACK!

CLICK!

CLICK!

C. L.S.

WSB

ward against itself but by hitting backward against the table? Either way might somersault it into the air with a chance of landing on its feet, which is what it wants. But which way does it use?

This is not a profound question, but the fact that there is complete professional disagreement on so readily observed a bit of behavior shows how much more careful observation and recording of beetle life remains to be done, both by professionals and amateurs.

The study of beetles is a hobby to which you can make contributions, corroborating the findings of others and offering new observations of your own — increasing your own pleasure in it as you help to extend the whole great field of knowledge. You "get the most" because the more you give, the more you get out of it.

So good luck and good beetle hunting!

A Final Bow
by Eleodes ~ ~ ~   *~ the Darkling*
                                Beetle
                        or Pinacate "Bug"
c. 1½ X L.S.   *of the S.W.-U.S.A.*

Index

Page numbers in italics refer to illustrations

Abdomen, 14, 28, 29, 70, *12*
African Goliath, 18
Ambrosia beetles, 74-76, *74*
American bean weevil, 90, *90*
Anobium punctatum DeGeer.
    See Furniture beetles
Anobium tessalatum. See
    Deathwatch beetles
Antennae, 22, 39, *12, 20*
Anthrenus museorum. See
    Museum beetles
Anthrenus scrophulariae. See
    Carpet beetles
Aphids, 88
Aquarium, preparation and
    care of, 114-118, *114*
Attraction to lights, 35, 37

Bacon beetle, 83, *85*
Balaninus rectus. See Nut
    weevils
Bark beetle. *See* Fir engraver
    beetles
Beautiful searcher, 92-93, *6, 94*
Beetle battles, 61, 72, *62*
Bess bugs, 69-71, *69*
Blister beetle, 154, *155*
Blood. *See* Circulation
Bombardier beetles, 91-92, *94*
Bookworms, 84, *84*
Brachinus stygicornis. See
    Bombardier beetles
Brain and nerves. *See* Nervous
    system
Bruchus rufimanus Boh. *See*
    American bean weevil
Bugs, defined, 87, *90*

Buprestis splendens. See
    Metallic wood borers
Burying beetles. *See* Sexton
    beetles

Calosoma calidum Fab. *See*
    Fiery hunter
Calosoma scrutator Fab. *See*
    Beautiful searcher
Calosoma sycophanta Linn., 93
Capricorns, 76, *84*
Carabidae, 90-93
Carbon dioxide (carbonic acid
    gas), 27, 79, 100
Carpet beetles, 83, *85*
Carrion beetles, 67, *65*
Chitin, 13, 28, 101
Cicindelidae. *See* Tiger beetles
Cigarette beetle, *84*
Circulation, 24-26, *20*
Click beetles, 154, 156, *155*
Coffee bugs. *See* Whirligig
    beetles
Collecting beetles
    equipment needed, 119, 122-
        125, 127-132, 134, 136, 142-
        145, *119, 123, 128, 130-131,
        144-145*
    exchanging specimens, 120,
        152
    identifying and classifying
        specimens, 148-153
    methods of capturing speci-
        mens, 125-140, *126, 134-
        135*
    methods of killing specimens,
        122-125

methods of mounting and
preserving specimens,
142-150, *145, 146-147, 151*
See also Aquarium
Colorado potato beetle, 85, *90*
Copris anaglypticus Say, 137,
138
Copris hispanus Linn. *See*
Spanish *Copris*
Copris lunaris Linn. *See* Moon
Copris
Copris tullius Oliv., 137
Crop, 21, 22, 23, *20*
Cucumber beetles, 89, *90*

Darkling beetles, 154, *156*
Deathwatch beetles, 82, *84*
Dermestes lardarius. See Bacon
beetle
Digestion, 21-24, *20*
Dineutes, 111, *103. See also*
Whirligig beetles
Dispersal, 43-44
Diving beetles, 96-97, 116, *98*
Drugstore beetle, *84*
Dung beetles, 51, 53, 60, *138*
Dynastes hercules L. *See*
Hercules beetles
Dytiscidae, 97-102, 114, 116,
133, 151, *98, 114, 151*

Earth borer beetles, 57-59, *54*
Eggs, 41-42
Epilachna borealis Fab. *See*
Cucumber beetles
Epilachna corrupta Muls. *See*
Mexican bean beetles
Epilachna varivestis Muls. *See*
Mexican bean beetles
Eyes, bifocal, 106, *102*
Eyes, simple and compound,
35-37, *36*

Feelers, 22, *20*
Feelings, 8, 12, 34, 39

Fiddle beetle, *6*
Fiery hunter, 93, *94*
Film, surface, 112
Fireflies, 37, 42, *38*
Fir engraver beetles, 73, *74*
Flight, method of, 15-18, 43, *16*
Flour beetles, 83, 141, 142, *84*
Fore-gut. *See* Proventriculus
Furniture beetles, 82, *84*

Ganglia, 31, 32, *20*
Geotrupid beetles, 57-59, *54*
Gills, 27, 29, *103*
Glowworms. *See* Fireflies
Goliathus goliathus Drury. *See*
African Goliath
Golofa beetle, *61*
Great black water beetle. *See*
Water scavenger
Great silver water beetle. *See*
Water scavenger
Ground beetles, 90-93, *94*
Gullet, 22, 23
Gyrinidae, 103-113, 114, *102-
103*
Gyrinus borealis lugens Lec.
See Whirligig beetles

Harpalus caliginosus Say. *See*
Murky ground beetle
Head, 13, *20*
Hearing, 22, 106
Heart, 24-25, 28, *20*
Hercules beetles, *62-63*
Hind-gut, 22, 24, *20*
Hister beetles, 154, *65, 155*
Hitchhikers, 43, *154*
Home museum. *See* Collecting
beetles
Horn bugs. *See* Bess bugs
Horns, 55, 57, 60-63, *61-63*
Hydrophilidae, 97-102, 116, *99*
Hylotrupes bajulus. See Old
house borer

Imagos, 59
Instinct and intelligence, 8-11,
    31-33

Japanese beetles, 32, 85, 91,
    125, 127, *85*
Jaws, 22-23, *12, 20*
June bugs, 85, 91, 125, 137, 146,
    148-149, *6, 85, 146*

Keel, 101, *99*

Lachnosterna fusca Frohl. *See*
    June bugs
Ladybird beetles, 87-90, 137,
    150, *90*
Ladybugs. *See* Ladybird beetles
Larvae, 27, 29, 39
Lasioderma serricorne Fab.
    See Cigarette beetle
Leaf beetles, *155*
Leaf-roller weevil, *155*
Leg breaking, 25
Leptinotarsa decemlineata Say.
    See Colorado potato beetle
Locusts, 43
Longhorns, 76, 77
Longicorns. *See* Longhorns
Lucanus dama Fab., 72, *71*
Lucanus elaphus Fab., 71-73, *71*
Lunary *Copris. See* Moon
    Copris
Lungs, 27

Mandibles, 23, 66, *12, 20, 94*
Maxillae, 23, *12, 20, 94*
May beetles. *See* June bugs
Meal worms, 83, 114, 141, *84,
    114*
Mealy bugs, 88
Metabolic water, 79-81
Metallic wood borers, 76-78, *78*
Metamorphosis, complete and
    incomplete, 39-41
Mexican bean beetles, 89, *90*

Mid-gut, 23, 24, *20*
Moon *Copris*, 57, *54*
Mormolyce phyllodes Hagenb.
    See Fiddle beetle
Murky ground beetle, *94*
Museum beetle, 83, *85*

Naming beetles, 44-47
Nervous system, 31-39, *20*
Net making, 127-132, *128, 130-
    133*
Nitrogen, 100
Nut weevil, *85*

Oil beetle, 154, *155*
Old house borer, 82, *84*
Onthophagus beetles, 57, *54*
Oxygen, 27-30, 100

Palpi (palps), 23, 39, *12, 20, 94*
Passalus cornutus Fab. *See* Bess
    bugs
Patent leather beetles. *See* Bess
    bugs
Peg bugs. *See* Bess bugs
Philotecnus nigricollis Lec., 46
Philotecnus ruficollis Lec., 46
Pin-borer beetle, *74*
Popilius disjunctus Illiger. *See*
    Bess bugs
Popillia japonica Newm. *See*
    Japanese beetles
Preserving larvae, 150, *151*
Propeller wings, *16*
Protozoans, 80
Proventriculus (gizzard), 23, *20*
Pselaphidae, 154, *155*
Pseudolucanus capreolus
    Linn., 72
Ptinid beetles, *84*
Ptinus brunneus. See Book-
    worms
Pupa and pupating, 40, *41*

Reference books, 152-153

Reproduction, 39-44, *20*
Respiration, 27-30, *20*
Round-headed apple tree
    borer, 76, *41*
Rove beetles, 67, 137, *65*

Saperda candida. See Round-
    headed apple tree borer
Scale insects, 88
Scarab beetles, 47-50, 51, 58, *48*
Scarabaeus sacer Linn. *See*
    Scarab beetles
Scavenger beetles, 8-9, 47-68
Scolytids, 73-76, *74*
Scolytus ventralis Lec. *See* Fir
    engraver beetles
Scuttlebugs. *See* Whirligig
    beetles
Sexton beetles, 64-68, *65*
Shot-hole borer, 81, *85*
Sitodrepa panicea. See Drug-
    store beetle
Skeleton and muscles, 13-21,
    12, 20
Smell, sense of, 22, 65, 88
Spanish *Copris,* 53-56, *54*
Spiracles, 28-30, 79, 81, 101, *20*
Squash eater, *90*
Stag beetles, 71-73, *71*
Stomach, 21, 22
Strength of insects, 14

Taxis, 35
*Tecnophilus croceicollis nigri-
    collis* Lec., 47
*Tecnophilus croceicollis rufi-
    collis* Lec., 47, *48*
Tenebrio molitor Linn. *See*
    Flour beetles

Thorax, 13, 28, 29, 31, 53, 58,
    62, 101, *12*
Tiger beetles, 25, 93-95, 139,
    140-141, *138*
Touch, sense of, 39, *20*
Tracheae, 27-28, 29, 30, 20
Tracheoles, 28
Tubes, 13, 28, *12, 20*
Tumblebugs, 50, 59, 139, *9, 51*

U. S. Dept. of Agriculture
    publications, 86, 149

Walking, method of, 15, *12*
Water beetles, 96-118, 141,
    98-99, 102-103
Water scavenger, 97-102, *99*
Water strider, 110
Weevils, 90, 97, 154, *85*
Whirligig beetles, 103-113, 116,
    103-104
  eyes of, 106, *103*
  maneuvers of, 107
  play of, 104-105
  sonar system of, 106
  swimming of, 111-113
Wing(s)
  braces (veins) of, 14, 19, 26,
    12
  covers, 18, 70, *12, 16*
  folding of, 18-21, *16*
Writes-My-Name. *See* Whirli-
    gig beetles

Xyleborus dispar Fab. *See* Pin-
    borer beetle
Xylobiops basillaris Say. *See*
    Shot-hole borer